KU-509-504

Biology of Reptiles

Th is book to be returned on c

2003

LIVERPOOL JMU LIBRARY

3 1111 00586 2246

TERTIARY LEVEL BIOLOGY

A series covering selected areas of biology at advanced undergraduate level. While designed specifically for course options at this level within Universities and Polytechnics, the series will be of great value to specialists and research workers in other fields who require a knowledge of the essentials of a subject.

Titles in the series:

Experimentation in Biology	Ridgman
Methods in Experimental Biology	Ralph
Visceral Muscle	Huddart and Hunt
Biological Membranes	Harrison and Lunt
Comparative Immunobiology	Manning and Turner
Water and Plants	Meidner and Sheriff
Biology of Nematodes	Croll and Matthews
An Introduction to Biological Rhythms	Saunders
Biology of Ageing	Lamb
Biology of Reproduction	Hogarth
An Introduction to Marine Science	Meadows and Campbell
Biology of Fresh Waters	Maitland
An Introduction to Developmental Biology	Ede
Physiology of Parasites	Chappell
Neurosecretion	Maddrell and Nordmann
Biology of Communication	Lewis and Gower
Population Genetics	Gale
Structure and Biochemistry of Cell Organelles	Reid
Developmental Microbiology	Peberdy
Genetics of Microbes	Bainbridge
Biological Functions of Carbohydrates	Candy
Endocrinology	Goldsworthy, Robinson and Mordue
The Estuarine Ecosystem	McLusky
Animal Osmoregulation	Rankin and Davenport
Molecular Enzymology	Wharton and Eisenthal
Environmental Microbiology	Grant and Long
The Genetic Basis of Development	Stewart and Hunt
Locomotion of Animals	Alexander
Animal Energetics	Brafield and Llewellyn

TERTIARY LEVEL BIOLOGY

Biology of Reptiles
An Ecological Approach

IAN F. SPELLERBERG. M.Sc., Ph.D., F.L.S.
Lecturer in Biology
University of Southampton

Blackie

Glasgow and London

Distributed in the USA by
Chapman and Hall
New York

Blackie & Son Limited,
Bishopbriggs, Glasgow G64 2NZ
Furnival House, 14–18 High Holborn, London WC1V 6BX

Distributed in the USA by
Chapman and Hall
in association with Methuen, Inc.
733 Third Avenue,
New York, N.Y. 10017

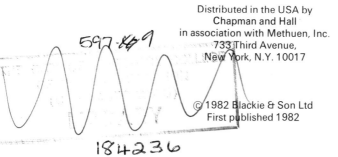

© 1982 Blackie & Son Ltd
First published 1982

All rights reserved.
No part of this publication may be reproduced,
stored in a retrieval system, or transmitted,
in any form or by any means,
electronic, mechanical, recording or otherwise,
without prior permission of the Publishers

British Library Cataloguing in Publication Data

Spellerberg, Ian F.
  Biology of reptiles. — (Tertiary level biology)
  1. Reptiles
  I. Title   II. Series
  597.9   QL641
  ISBN 0-216-91257-1
  ISBN 0-216-91256-3 Pbk

Library of Congress Cataloging in Publication Data

Spellerberg, Ian F.
  Biology of reptiles.
  (Tertiary level biology)
  Bibliography: p.
  Includes index.
  1. Reptiles.   I. Title.   II. Series.
  QL665.S63   597.9   81-22457
  ISBN 0-412-00161-6 (Chapman and Hall)   AACR2
  ISBN 0-412-00171-3 (Chapman and Hall: pbk.)

Filmset by Advanced Filmsetters (Glasgow) Ltd

Printed in Great Britain by
Thomson Litho Ltd, East Kilbride, Scotland

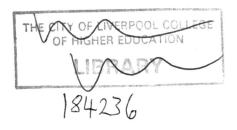

THE CITY OF LIVERPOOL COLLEGE
OF HIGHER EDUCATION
LIBRARY

184236

Preface

This short book on the biology of reptiles is written primarily for the advanced undergraduate. It is hoped that it will also be a useful source for the specialist not familiar with reptile biology.

Since the interaction of an organism with its environment determines its morphology, physiology and behaviour, I have adopted an ecological approach with the aim of providing a more functional interpretation of the material. An ecological approach (with relevant physiology) fills an obvious gap, because other small books on the biology of reptiles concentrate either on comparative anatomy and palaeontology, or on zoogeography and ecology. With little room for literary embellishments, I have resisted the temptation of adopting an encyclopaedic style. Throughout, the aim has been to describe the essentials of reptile biology and to introduce new and stimulating ideas which may be of interest to undergraduates and research workers.

The book commences with a synthesis of recent literature on the evolution and phylogeny of reptiles, which is followed by a comprehensive account of reptile functional anatomy. Where relevant, an ecological interpretation of reptile form and function is included. The patterns of reptile distribution and species abundance are then described and illustrated with examples from both America and Europe. The essentials of reproduction and development in reptiles provide a basis for a discussion of reproductive strategies. This is followed by two ecological chapters, in which the abiotic and biotic relations of reptiles receive a comprehensive and critical appraisal. These chapters incorporate the results of recent studies on niche theory and community ecology, to which research on reptiles has made a major contribution. There is much overlap between ecology and behaviour, but a separate chapter on reptile behaviour contains significant material on the patterns and analysis of animal behaviour. The final chapter brings together some of the literature relating to the exploitation and conservation of reptiles.

At this level, students do well not to take statements on trust, but to consider the information in the light of all available and relevant material. For this reason I have thought it important to include alternative interpretations where possible. However, different authors emphasize different aspects of the subject, and there may be errors of judgement in this as in any other text. In this respect, I would welcome comments and advice.

I am indebted to Professor A. d'A. Bellairs, Dr F. S. Billett, Dr R. J. Putman and Dr R. A. Avery for their encouragement and expert advice. My thanks to all those who assisted in the preparation of the manuscript, especially Nick Smith, Raymond Cornick, Dawn Trenchard, Sally Johnson and Karen Spellerberg. Care has been taken to ensure that full acknowledgment is given to work which is not my own, and I am grateful for material from scientists throughout the world.

I.F.S.

Contents

CHAPTER ONE

ORIGINS, RADIATION AND CLASSIFICATION OF REPTILES

1.1 Continental drift and origins of reptiles

The first reptiles evolved when the continental land masses were incorporated in one southern super-continent. During the Permian the outline of some continents appeared, but it is thought that at about 200 million years ago (during the Triassic) there was still a universal continent (Dietz and Holden, 1970). By 180 million years ago (at the end of the Triassic) the northern groups of continents (Laurasia) separated from the southern groups of continents (Gondwana): the African–South American land masses began to separate from the Antarctic–Australian land masses. India separated from the southern group at the end of the Triassic and collided with Asia during the Cretaceous. Good evidence for a past link between Australia, New Zealand and South America via the Antarctic continent can be seen in the distribution of several groups of organisms; for example, the southern beech *Nothofagus* and the arthropod *Peripatus*. In addition, a fossil of the therapsid *Lystrosaurus* (an aquatic mammal-like reptile) was found in Antarctica during an expedition there in 1969.

It was towards the close of the Devonian period (about 350–400 million years ago), when the climate was warm, that some amphibians evolved from an airbreathing fish—probably a rhipidistian crossopterygian. From these creatures, ancient and modern amphibian groups evolved, and more importantly the more fully terrestrial vertebrates arose. During the Carboniferous (about 280–350 million years ago) the amphibians had a widespread distribution, and before the end of that period the ancestral reptiles had appeared. During this time the world's continental masses were probably in apposition. It must be emphasized, however, that reptiles did not appear suddenly; there may have been a diphyletic or possibly even

1

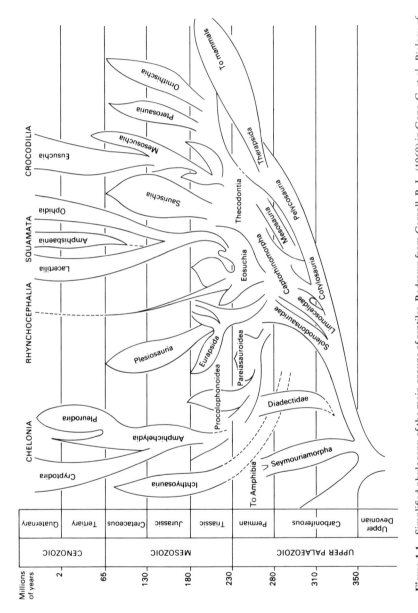

Figure 1.1 Simplified phylogeny of the main groups of reptiles. Redrawn from Carroll, R. L. (1969) in Gans, C. et al., *Biology of the Reptilia*, Vol. 1, Academic Press, pp. 1–44.

a polyphyletic origin. Throughout many millions of years vertebrate animals with both amphibian and reptilian features slowly achieved a partial then fully terrestrial existence. Some forms survived, many were to become extinct, and a few evolved along very different lines.

The Triassic was an important period, since by then the terrestrial reptiles were numerous and the first marine reptiles and the dinosaurs were beginning to appear. About 65 million years ago (by the end of the Cretaceous) Madagascar separated from Africa, and the major continents were well separated, although Australia and Antarctica may still have been linked.

1.2   Origins and evolution of reptiles

The precise nature of the origins of the primitive reptiles and the characteristics of the ancestors of the class Reptilia during the Late Carboniferous (Pennsylvanian) and Early Permian have been keenly debated for decades (see Ginsburg, 1970). A well-researched and balanced account of reptile origins has been put forward by Carroll (1969), who concluded that the Captorhinomorpha (a suborder of the order Cotylosauria) includes the most primitive reptiles and the potential ancestors of the entire class (Figure 1.1). The earliest known reptile is the small *Romeriscus* from Cape Breton Island in Nova Scotia. Unfortunately we know nothing of the environment in which it lived. Like the other very early tetrapods it was a small animal, with a skull of about 6 cm in length. Further back in time the Seymouriamorpha probably branched off the phylogenetic line leading to the ancestors of the Reptilia. A much-disputed animal is *Seymouria* (about 55 cm in length); although sometimes accepted as having both amphibian and reptilian features, it cannot be considered as a remnant of an early group which was ancestral to the reptiles. The early Solenodonsauridae is a family (sometimes placed within the Captorhinomorpha family) which Carroll believes is close to the ancestry of most, if not all reptiles. Some of the earliest reptiles known, including the earliest solenodonsaurids, come from Joggins, Nova Scotia, where they were found within stumps of upright lycopods. Once buried, these trees with centres rotted-out formed pitfall traps for the new terrestrial animals.

The surviving evidence for the nature and origin of early reptiles is scant, but we now know that during the Permian there was a radiation of the Captorhinomorpha and a trend towards a larger size. The order Pelycosauria contained early representatives of a line leading to the mammals (Figure 1.1). There is some dispute as to whether the emergence of tetrapods on to land was a slow or rapid process following the origin of the amniote egg. One of the most interesting discussions on the spectacular spread of the terrestrial tetrapods during the Late Permian comes from Olson (1976), who considers that invasion was rapid and related to alterations in community structure. The early small reptiles were dependent on insects and Olson has drawn attention to the temporal and a broad ecological correlation of adaptive radiation of insects and reptiles, which may indicate coevolution. At about the same time the semi-aquatic (followed by terrestrial), herbivorous reptiles emerged, and Olson considers the latter to be an essential factor facilitating the occupancy of new terrestrial life zones. The larger plant-eating reptiles seemed then to outnumber terrestrial carnivores, compared with circumstances existing during the Early Permian. Olson also suggests that the biomass provided by reptilian herbivores soon became a basis for a reptile-dominated ecosystem, with carnivorous reptiles at the apex of the trophic pyramid.

The terrestrial reptiles flourished, and the dinosaurs and the large marine reptiles existed, during the Triassic (about 180–230 million years ago). The Archosaurian orders, including the larger dinosaurs, became dominant forms during the Jurassic (about 130–180 million years ago) and during the same period some reptiles took to the air. Interestingly enough, toothed birds (*Archaeopteryx*, which was less than 30 cm in length) probably evolved from reptile stock at about that time. In the early Cretaceous (about 125 million years ago) there was a great array of reptiles, many with specialized forms. Then, quite suddenly in geological terms, towards the end of the Cretaceous (about 70 million years ago) there was a world-wide extinction of more than 34 % of the reptile orders, most of which were the larger Archosaurian forms. Although the earliest known snakes, such as *Dinilysia*, came from the Late Cretaceous of Patagonia (Carroll, 1969), there was possibly a considerable adaptive radiation over a short period of time, particularly in the Eocene and Palaeocene (about 38–65 million years ago) when the ancient mammals were dominant.

Of the three major reptilian groups (Figure 1.1) known from the close of the Carboniferous and the Permian, the Captorhinomorphs are close to the ancestry of all advanced reptile groups. The Pelycosaurs were primitive mammal-like reptiles and the diadectids were a specialized group which generally had terrestrial adaptations, but their associations are little understood. The crocodiles evolved from the thecodonts early in the Triassic and have changed little in general body form. Both the Squamata and the Rhynchocephalia evolved from the eosuchians (an extinct order of the subclass Lepidosauria) in the Permian, but the latter were to evolve along a separate line for about 190 million years. There is considerable speculation regarding the ancestry of the Chelonia. Carroll (1969) has suggested that they probably arose from the same stock as the Permian–Triassic procolophonids and pareiasaurs in the late Permian or early Triassic and that this stock had common ancestry with the eosuchians.

But why, out of 17 known reptile orders, have only 4 orders survived? It is a poor legacy from what was once a flourishing and spectacular array of dominant animals. Many theories have been offered. Some suggest that gravity increased and the larger reptiles collapsed on themselves, but most identify climate as a major factor (see Chapter 5). How could a change in climate act directly on the reptiles of that time? One particularly interesting idea concerns the coevolution of the reptiles and angiosperms and, particularly, chemical changes in the flora during the Late Cretaceous. Swain (1976) has suggested that flowering plants developed the ability to produce unique hydrolysable tannins, which were more efficient deterrents against herbivores than those present in the lower plants, and this reduced the amount of palatable food available to all herbivores. Angiosperms synthesize many toxic alkaloids (largely as a result of plant–insect interactions) and it is known that these chemicals are less easily detected by reptiles than by mammals. Swain cites a number of references for this, and it is tempting to conclude that the archosaurs ("ruling reptiles") were poisoned. He also suggests that the toxic alkaloids interfered with physiological activities; for example there may be a connection between the observed thinning of egg shells of the Late Cretaceous ceratopians and the production of toxic substances by the flowering plants. If the angiosperm–reptile coevolution did lead in part to the extinction of reptiles, it may therefore have provided an opportunity for the small mammals of the time to evolve and take the place of the reptiles as the dominant animals. There are many "buts" to this and other theories; nevertheless there seems no doubt that a change in climate was directly or indirectly related to the mass extinction of the dinosaurs.

1.3 Phylogeny and classification of reptiles

In the generalized phylogeny of the major reptilian groups (see Figure 1.1) we see two important early evolutionary trends: the radiation of the Captorhinomorpha and the separation of the Pelycosauria. There were clearly two great branches, one leading to the Synapsida or mammal-like reptiles and one following on from the Captorhinomorpha. The structure of the skull forms a basis for the main anatomical difference between members of these two groups and also for reptile subclasses. Criteria used in the systematic classification of the reptiles include the number and position of temporal openings and also the vertebral structure. Openings in the temporal region (Figure 2.4) resulted from the evolution of the jaw muscles and a need for better attachment and arrangement. Early researchers, however, based their classification on the position and nature of the vertebral arches and not the temporal openings, as is seen in names such as Anapsid and Synapsid containing the Greek root "apse" or arch. The classification used by Romer and Parsons (1977) has been used as a basis for the following account.

Subclass Synapsida (all extinct)

These were the mammal-like reptiles with a single lateral temporal fossa (opening) on each side of the skull. It was thought at one time that the single fossa was formed by fusion of the two fossae present in the diapsid

Figure 1.2 Examples of extinct synapsid reptiles: (*a*) *Cynognathus* (Therapsid), about the size of a wolf; (*b*) *Dimetrodon* (Pelycosaur), three or more metres in length; (*c*) *Lycaenops* (Therapsid), about the size of a large dog; (*d*) *Ophiacodon* (primitive Pelycosaur), about 10 m in length. (*a*) and (*b*) redrawn from Fenton, C. L. (1966), *Tales told by Fossils*, Doubleday; (*c*) redrawn from Colbert, E. H. (1965), *The Age of Reptiles*, Weidenfeld and Nicolson; (*d*) redrawn from Romer, A. S. and Parsons, T. S. (1977), *The Vertebrate Body* (5th ed.), W. B. Saunders.

reptiles, thus resulting in the inappropriate name for the group. The Synapsids include two important orders: Pelycosauria and Therapsida. The pelycosaurs were a dominant group of reptiles and a well-known example was *Dimetrodon* (Figure 1.2), about 3 m in length and characterized by the large dorsal "sail" which could have been used for temperature regulation. Most were carnivorous with sharply pointed teeth. The other order, Therapsida, was also very successful. These are called the advanced "mammal-like" reptiles and there are at least three suborders. One well-known example is the predaceous *Cynognathus*, about the size of a wolf, with large canines and cheek teeth possessing accessory cusps. It had many features which brought it towards the mammalian condition and it has been suggested that *Cynognathus* was homeothermic (Colbert, 1965).

Subclass Anapsida

These include the oldest known reptile forms: the temporal region of the skull typically lacked the fenestrae. Three orders are usually recognized: the extinct Cotylosauria or stem reptiles from the Carboniferous and

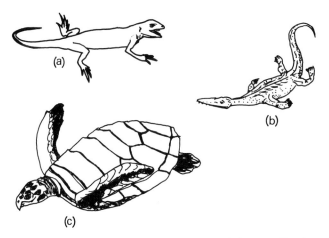

(a)

(b)

(c)

Figure 1.3 Examples of extinct anapsid reptiles: (*a*) *Cephalerpeton* (Cotylosaur), small primitive lizard-like "stem" reptile whose affinities are much debated; (*b*) *Mesosaurus* (Mesosaur), about one metre in length; (*c*) *Archelon ischyros* (Upper Cretaceous chelonian), about six metres in length. (*a*) redrawn from Romer and Parsons (1977) after Carroll, R. L. and Baird, D. (1968) *Am. Mus. Novit.*, **2337**, 1–50; (*b*) redrawn from Goin, C. J. *et al.* (1978) *Introduction to Herpetology* (3rd ed.), W. H. Freeman; (*c*) redrawn from Grzimek, H. C. B. (1975) *Animal Life Encyclopaedia*, Vol. 6, Reptiles, Van Nostrand Reinhold.

Permian; the extinct Mesosauria; and the Chelonia (Testudines). The order Mesosauria includes freshwater forms, probably fish-eaters, and it seems that they became extinct well before the end of the Permian. *Mesosaurus* is a well-known example and fossils of this animal have been found in South Africa and South America. The Chelonia probably had very early origins from the primitive Cotylosaurs and five suborders are usually recognized. They lack the temporal openings, but the most extraordinary development was the shell. The shell of primitive turtles was originally not flat, but highly arched, and contained many bony elements, no longer present in turtles today. The Chelonia flourished in both species richness and in adaptive diversity. There was also a considerable range in size: one species from the Pleistocene in Australia, *Meiolania*, was a large horned turtle with a skull about 50 cm wide; another from the Upper Cretaceous of the United States was the large marine turtle *Archelon ischyros* about 6 m in length (Figure 1.3). Although we usually regard the Chelonia as typically slow-moving animals, those forms which returned to an aquatic existence (marine turtles) are by far the swiftest of all reptiles. Of the twelve living turtle families, many are ancient in origin, most appearing in the Jurassic and the Late Cretaceous.

Subclass Lepidosauria

These are primitive reptiles or generalized relatives of the diapsid form without archosaur specializations. Typically they have two temporal openings but these have become reduced in the more specialized forms; although the temporal openings may be obscured they can be traced to forms that were diapsid. Three orders are recognized. The Eosuchia are all extinct; there is one surviving species of the order Rhynchocephalia; and the order Squamata has by far the largest number of living species, about 6000.

The Eosuchians appeared in the Mid- to Upper Permian and the Eosuchian skull was like that of an advanced Cotylosaur except for its diapsid temporal region. The Eosuchians are ancestral to the lizards and two relatively little-known families are recognized. *Youngina* is perhaps the best known from a family found in the upper Permian of Europe and South Africa.

Members of the ancient order Rhynchocephalia (primitive lepidosaurians, so called because the upper jaw has a small overhanging beak) have diapsid skulls. Although never a very large group, it did have a widespread distribution including North America, Europe, eastern Asia

Figure 1.4 The tuatara (*Sphenodon*) of New Zealand: adults grow to about 62 cm in length. Drawn by P. G. Jack.

and South Africa. The one surviving species (*Sphenodon punctatus*, Figure 1.4) is restricted to islands off New Zealand.

The Squamata (suborders Lacertilia, Serpentes, Amphisbaenia) are the most successful living reptiles. Generally the skull of the Lacertilia has lost one temporal opening. In some lizards the remaining temporal opening is covered by neighbouring elements, and in burrowing forms there is a reduction and a loss of the postorbital and squamosal bones. The Eosuchian *Prolacerta* from the Triassic with its progressive reduction of the lower temporal arches acts as an important link between the Eosuchians and the lizards.

In the suborder Ophidia (Serpentes), both temporal openings are secondarily lost and the upper temporal arch is missing. With the loss of the lower arch there is a broad open area and a movable quadrate. As the lower jaw articulates with the quadrate this condition is particularly advantageous for swallowing large prey. The snakes have a relatively recent origin (early or middle Mesozoic), and it is generally believed that the loss and reduction of limbs and girdles evolved as a result of adaptations for burrowing. Alternatively, limb reduction may have been a perfection of crypsis by predator selection. The origin of snakes has proved difficult to establish, and the lack of fossil material has added to the difficulties of classification, but particularly useful contributions to the classification of snakes may be found in Underwood (1967) and Dunson (1975).

The suborder Amphisbaenia (sometimes referred to as an infraorder

Figure 1.5   An amphisbaenian, *Blanus cinereus*, from Spain. This species reaches up to about 25 cm in length but is usually much smaller. Drawn by P. G. Jack.

Annulata) is a group of highly specialized burrowing animals (Figure 1.5). The temporal arches are generally lost and so also are the postfrontal, squamosal and postorbital bones. The skull is very solid and heavily ossified, with relatively few large teeth. Although these animals differ from the lizards and snakes in a number of respects, they do show affinities with them, for example in the arrangement of the endocrine glands, the architecture of the brain and the path of some of the blood vessels (Francis, 1977; Gans, 1978).

Subclass Archosauria

These are the diapsid reptiles which usually have extra cranial fenestrae. Some are well adapted for bipedal locomotion. The Archosaurs were the "ruling reptiles" of the Mesozoic. Of the five recognized orders (Thecodontia, Crocodilia, Pterosaura, Saurischia, Ornithischia), representatives from only one, the rather aberrant Crocodilia, survive today. The order Thecodontia includes the basically primitive reptiles which were central to the evolution of the higher vertebrates. As well as giving rise to the dinosaurs, they were also ancestral to the birds. Many were large and bulky animals, but typical forms were small, with a tendency for elongated hind limbs and a modified hip structure. Representatives of the Pseudosuchia (a suborder of the Thecodontia), such as *Euparkeria*, arose in the Triassic. They were small carnivorous reptiles with long slim skulls and sharp teeth along the jaw edges. Triassic representatives of the suborder Phytosauria are the particularly interesting aquatic crocodile-like Thecodonts. Widely distributed in the northern hemisphere, their general body form suggests a convergent evolution with the Crocodilia.

Figure 1.6 Examples of extinct Archosaurian reptiles: (*a*) *Euparkeria* (Thecodont) up to about 75 cm in length; (*b*) *Metriorhynchus* (crocodilian, suborder Mesosuchia) between two and three metres in length; (*c*) *Pteranodon* (pterosaur) with wingspan of about 7 metres; (*d*) *Iguanodon* (Ornithischian) up to about 9 metres in length. (*a*), (*c*) and (*d*) redrawn from British Museum Publication (1979) *Dinosaurs and their Living Relatives*, Cambridge University Press. (*b*) redrawn from Fenton, C. L. (1966) *Tales told by Fossils*, Doubleday.

The crocodilians evolved from primitive thecodonts during the Middle Triassic, and of the five suborders recognized, four are now extinct. The suborder Mesosuchia, the central stock of the crocodilians, was a very large, widespread group. Some examples, such as *Metriorhynchus* (Figure 1.6), found in the middle Jurassic to lower Cretaceous, were marine forms with fish-like tails and paddle-shaped limbs.

The order Pterosauria (Pterodactyla) were spectacular gliding or soaring maritime reptiles. In some ways the skeleton had been modified in a manner analogous to that of birds. It was light, thin and pneumatic and the forelimbs had an elongated fourth digit supporting the membranous patagium. Typically the first three digits were small and clawed, while the fifth was absent. The pterosaurs (such as *Pterodactylus* and *Pteranodon*) evolved from the Thecodontia during the Triassic, and by the Upper Cretaceous had a very wide distribution, including Australia (Molnar and Thulborn, 1980). The order Saurischia (together with the Ornithischia) are

the spectacular mesozoic creatures often collectively called the "dinosaurs". Although the well-known representatives were very large animals,
many forms were small and generally there was great variation and
specialization. The Saurischia were "reptile-like" dinosaurs with a triradiate pelvis (Figure 2.5), and the forelimbs were shorter than the
hindlimbs. There are two suborders: the Theropoda, mainly carnivorous
dinosaurs, and the Sauropodomorpha, generally quadrupedal amphibious
herbivores. The Theropoda appeared in the Triassic and were probably the
earliest true dinosaurs; they are epitomized by the huge Jurassic carno-
saurian dinosaurs such as *Tyrannosaurus* (14 m in length) and *Allosaurus*
(10 m in length). They had a wide distribution and a notable adaptive
radiation. Some of the Sauropodomorpha, such as *Brachiosaurus*, *Bronto-
saurus* and *Diplodocus*, were probably the largest and heaviest of all land
animals. One of the largest known dinosaurs, *Brachiosaurus*, weighed at
least 50 tonnes and was about 24 m in total length. While the limb bones
were massive, it is astonishing that they could support the weight of such
large dinosaurs. The bones do seem to have been strong enough for the
animals to move about without the support of water, as long as these
reptiles did not take excessively long steps.

The now extinct animals in the order Ornithischia were the bird-like
herbivorous dinosaurs with a tetraradiate pelvis (Figure 2.5), essentially
like that retained in modern birds. The order contains a variety of animals,
and is the second great group of dinosaurs which evolved from the
Thecodontia. Although most had the pelvic girdle and the hind limbs
adapted for bipedal locomotion, some had reverted to quadrupedal
locomotion. Of the four suborders, the Ornithopoda include such forms as
Iguanodon (about 3 m in length) which was abundant in the upper Jurassic
and lower Cretaceous. The primitive forms gave rise to the common,
amphibious and specialized "duck-billed" dinosaurs or hadrosaurids. The
Stegosauria, which include the slow-moving heavily armoured
Stegosaurus, about the size of an elephant, were quadrupedal forms living
during the Jurassic and lower Cretaceous. The suborder Ankylosauria,
present during the Cretaceous, comprised heavily armoured forms with
interesting overlapping layers of bony plates. Their short broad skulls had
the basic elements but were reinforced with additional plating of polygonal
bones. Finally, the suborder Ceratopsia, the quadrupedal rhinoceros-like
horned dinosaurs, included many forms with large skulls with extensions
of the parietals and squamosal bones, forming a frill of bone over the neck.
Well-known and often-illustrated representatives such as *Triceratops* grew
to a length of about 6 m.

Subclass Euryapsida (Parapsida, Synaptosauria)

This extinct group includes a diverse and possibly unrelated group of reptiles (Figure 1.7), with a single dorsal temporal opening on each side of the skull. The classification and the phylogeny of this group is much debated. Romer and Parsons (1977) list four orders: Araeoscelidia (Protorosauria), Sauropterygia, Placodontia, and Ichthyosauria (the last of these is now placed in a separate subclass). The Araeoscelidia include various terrestrial forms, most of which were lizard-like slender reptiles, and there is some debate as to their relationships. The Sauropterygia were amphibious or marine reptiles with paddle-like limbs. Included in this order is the very successful group of plesiosaurs which may have competed with the equally successful ichthyosaurs. Sometimes more than 15 m in length, the Plesiosaurs had very long necks and short heads, and were widely distributed. Their dentition was isodont with elongate teeth suitable for their piscivorous diet.

There are many romantic descriptions of plesiosaur-like animals. The Loch Ness Monster, for example, has been likened to a plesiosaur and it is tempting to believe in the existence of this monster which has been given

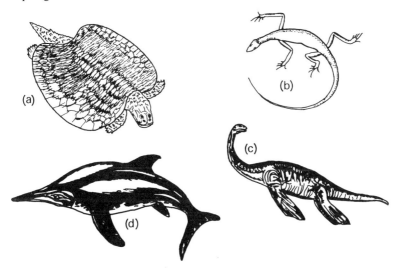

Figure 1.7 Examples of extinct Euryapsid reptiles: (*a*) *Henodus* (Placodont) just over one metre in length; (*b*) *Araeoscelis* (Araeoscelid), small and lizard-like; (*c*) *Plesiosaurus* (Sauropterygia), up to about 3 metres in length; (*d*) *Ichthyosaurus* (subclass Ichthyopterygia) about one and a half metres in length. (*a*) redrawn from Charig, A. (1979) *A New Look at Dinosaurs*, Heinemann; (*b*) redrawn from Williston, S. W. (1914) *J. Geol.*, **22**, 364–419; (*d*) redrawn from British Museum Publication (1979) *Dinosaurs and their Living Relatives*.

the name *Nessiteras rhombopteryx* (Scott and Rines, 1975). A much-published photograph of what appears to be a plesiosaur-like neck and head emerging from the water of Loch Ness is in fact an enlarged part of a photograph of an otter's tail—taken as the animal dived. Sadly, there is no material evidence to confirm that plesiosaur-like animals exist in Loch Ness or elsewhere.

The order Placodontia (e.g. *Henodus*, Figure 1.7) was a small group of Triassic armoured marine animals that could crush and eat molluscs. They had a heavily-built jaw with flattened palatine teeth, which were used as crushing plates. The last order, Ichthyosauria (here ranked as a subclass Ichthyopterygia) were a highly specialized group of marine reptiles. In general body form they paralleled the mammalian porpoises in their marine adaptations. The teeth were generally numerous, conical and sharply pointed. There were five families of Ichthyosaurs and fossil remains of these animals have been found in Jurassic and Cretaceous deposits of both hemispheres.

1.4   Taxonomy and systematic classification of living reptiles

The temporal openings and other features of the skull have formed an important basis for the systematic classification of reptiles, although more recently less emphasis has been put on these features. In general, skeletal characteristics are of taxonomic importance and often provide a good basis for the classification of reptiles at lower levels such as orders and families. A biochemical approach to the study of reptile phylogeny has also been developed. Some results can provide broad guidelines for reptilian systematics at higher taxonomic levels, for instance by using immuno-logical relationships derived from lactic dehydrogenase data. For example, research by Gorman *et al.* (1971) revealed that cross-reactivity studies with the albumins of some crocodilians fits with the suggestion that rate of albumin evolution in crocodilians has been similar to that in iguanids, and that as much albumin evolution has occurred in the iguanids as in mammalian orders.

Another parameter used to yield information on relationships is karyotypic data. Basically, a description of an organism's chromosome complement is the karyotype and the information is usually presented as records of the metaphase chromosomes, arranged by pairs in order of decreasing length. For example in iguanid lizards, a basic formula is six pairs of metacentric chromosomes (centromere midway between two ends) and 12 pairs of microchromosomes (Matthey, 1970).

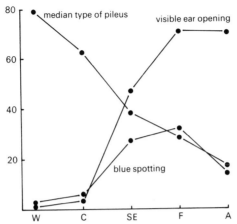

Figure 1.8   Relative frequencies of the blue-spotted morph, the visible ear opening, and the median type of pileus of *Anguis fragilis* from west to east in Europe. W = western and southwestern Europe, C = central Europe, SE = southeastern Europe, F = Finland, A = Asia Minor plus Persia. Redrawn from Voipio, P. (1962) *Ann. Zool. Soc. "Vanamo"*, **23**, 1–20.

Geographic variation may be continuous so that individuals can be scored in a series which shows the gradual change in characteristics. An example of a polymorphism with distinct groups or morphs has been described for the legless lizard, *Anguis fragilis*: the blue spotting (although very rare in females it is not sex-linked), visible ear opening and head shield patterns are the features used by Voipio in his 1962 study (Figure 1.8). A further interesting example of colour pattern variation was described by Camin and Ehrlich (1958) for island water snakes (*Natrix sipedon*) on the islands of Lake Erie. The skin pattern type of these snakes from the islands ranged through several classes from unbanded to banded. It seems that strong selection has produced a shift towards unbanded pattern types on the islands, while constant migration from the mainland has maintained "banded" genes in the island gene pools. The banded snakes on the limestone areas of the islands are very conspicuous and it is suggested that predation by gulls and other birds could be a principal selective influence.

Variation within a species which has a wide geographical distribution, such as *Podarcis sicula* (the Italian wall lizard) can be a basis for the recognition of subspecies. There are well over 40 island subspecies of *P. sicula* and classification is based on osteological features, hemipenial characters, external morphology, colour patterns, and chromosomes and allozyme variation.

Recognition of subspecies has sometimes been based largely on subjective discrimination of a few colour pattern characteristics. In addition to the possibility of many subspecies being recognized, erroneous conclusions may be reached in connection with boundaries between clinal subspecies. Examination of racial affinities and geographic variation can in some instances be more usefully examined with multivariate morphometrics. This method has been used on several European reptiles (Clover, 1979; Thorpe, 1980) including *P. sicula*. Using this method it has been found that this species segregates into two groups, one from the northern islands and one from the southern islands. Clover suggests that gene flow and natural selection (rather than genetic drift), together with post-pleistocene changes in sea level and the topography of the Adriatic basin, has caused these patterns. There seems no doubt that patterns of population differentiation can be obscured by the recognition of a large number of subspecies whereas the use of multivariate morphometrics reveals patterns which can be related to geological and climatic history (Thorpe, 1980). The use of multivariate morphometrics to investigate variation also provides a basis for the understanding of speciation mechanisms.

Families of the living reptiles (with minor reference to the extinct groups, to suborder) are listed below, providing a basis for discussion in the subsequent chapters. The classification of extinct and living reptiles is a topic of great dispute, but the system used here (although simplified) seems to be generally popular. Infraorder names have been omitted.

Subclass Synapsida
  Order Pelycosauria: extinct Carboniferous and Permian forms.
  Order Therapsida: extinct advanced mammal-like forms.
Subclass Anapsida
  Order Cotylosauria: extinct primitive stem reptiles including the suborder Captorhinomorpha.
  Order Mesosaura: extinct fresh water fish-eaters.
  Order Chelonia (= Testudinata)
    Suborder Proganochelyoidea: extinct.
    Suborder Amphichelydia: extinct.
    Suborder Pleurodira: the side-necked turtles.
      Family Pelomedusidae: e.g. *Pelomedusa, Podocnemis.*
      Family Chelidae: e.g. *Chelus, Platemys.*
    Suborder Cryptodira (modern turtles)
      Family Emydidae: pond turtles etc.: *Emys, Chrysemys.*
      Family Testudinidae: true tortoises, e.g. *Testudo, Gopherus.*
      Family Platysternidae: the big-headed tortoise, *Platysternon.*
      Family Chelydridae: snapping turtles, e.g. *Chelydra, Macroclemys.*
      Family Kinosternidae: musk turtles and mud terrapins, e.g. *Kinosternon, Sternotherus.*
      Family Dermatemydidae: Central American river turtle, *Dermatemys.*

Family Cheloniidae: marine turtles (hawksbill, loggerhead and green turtles), e.g. *Chelonia, Lepidochelys.*
Family Dermochelyidae: the leathery turtle, *Dermochelys.*
Family Carettochelyidae: large New Guinea river turtle, *Carettochelys.*
Family Trionychidae: soft-shelled turtles, e.g. *Trionyx, Cycloderma.*
Subclass Lepidosauria
Order Eosuchia: extinct.
Order Rhynchocephalia
Family Sphenodontidae: the tuatara, *Sphenodon.*
Order Squamata
Suborder Lacertilia (Sauria)
Family Gekkonidae: the geckos, e.g. *Hemidactylus, Gehyra.*
Family Pygopodidae: scale-footed lizards, e.g. *Pygopus.*
Family Xantusiidae: night lizards, e.g. *Xantusia.*
Family Dibamidae: a very small group of Old World burrowing lizards, e.g. *Dibamus.*
Family Anelytropsidae: Mexican blind lizard, e.g. *Anelytropsis.*
Family Iguanidae: iguanas, anolids and basilisks, e.g. *Sceloporus, Uma, Phrynosoma, Iguana, Basiliscus, Anolis.*
Family Agamidae: flying, rainbow and moloch lizards, e.g. *Agama, Amphibolurus, Moloch.*
Family Chamaeleontidae: the chamaeleons, e.g. *Chamaeleo, Brookesia.*
Family Scincidae: the skinks, e.g. *Tiliqua, Scincus, Eumeces, Mabuya, Sphenomorphus, Leiolopisma.*
Family Lacertidae: the true lizards, e.g. *Lacerta, Podarcis.*
Family Teiidae: whiptail lizards, e.g. *Cnemidophorus, Tupinambis.*
Family Feylinidae: small, burrowing, limbless and skink-like, e.g. *Feylinia.*
Family Cordylidae: girdled and plated lizards, e.g. *Gerrhosaurus.*
Family Anguidae: slow worms, "glass snakes" or legless lizards, and alligator lizards, e.g. *Anguis, Gerrhonotus, Ophisaurus.*
Family Anniellidae: the burrowing slow-worm, *Anniella.*
Family Xenosauridae: crocodile lizards and strange lizards, e.g. *Xenosaurus, Shinisaurus.*
Family Varanidae: monitor lizards, e.g. *Varanus.*
Family Helodermatidae: the Gila monster, *Heloderma.*
Family Lanthanotidae: the earless monitors, *Lanthanotus.*
Suborder Amphisbaenia
Family Bipedidae: worm lizards, e.g. *Bipes.*
Family Amphisbaenidae: the amphisbaenians, e.g. *Blanus.*
Family Trogonophidae: sharp-tailed worm lizards, e.g. *Trogonophis.*
Family Rhineuridae: Florida worm lizard, *Rhineura.*
Suborder Ophidia (= Serpentes)
Family Anomalepididae: blind snake, *Anomalepis.*
Family Typhlopidae: blind snakes, e.g. *Typhlops.*
Family Leptotyphlopidae: slender blind snakes or thread snakes, e.g. *Leptotyphlops.*
Family Anilidae: cylinder snakes, e.g. *Anilius.*
Family Uropeltidae: shieldtail snakes, e.g. *Uropeltis.*
Family Boidae: boas and pythons, e.g. *Boa, Python.*
Family Xenopeltidae: sunbeam snake, *Xenopeltis.*
Family Acrochordidae: wart-snakes, e.g. *Acrochordus.*
Family Colubridae: colubrid snakes, e.g. *Coluber, Coronella, Natrix.*
Family Elapidae: the elapid snakes (cobras, mambas, coral snakes etc.), e.g. *Ophiophagus, Dendroaspis, Calliophis, Naja.*
Family Viperidae: adders, true vipers, pit vipers, e.g. *Vipera, Crotalus.*

Subclass Archosauria
    Order Thecodontia: extinct.
    Order Crocodilia (= Loricata)
        Family Crocodylidae: crocodiles and alligators, e.g. *Crocodylus*, *Alligator*, *Caiman*.
        Family Gavialidae: the charial or gavial, e.g. *Gavialis*.
    Order Pterosauria: extinct flying reptiles.
    Order Saurischia: extinct reptile-like dinosaurs.
    Order Ornithischia: extinct bird-like dinosaurs.
Subclass Euryapsida
    Order Araeoscelidia: extinct various terrestrial forms.
    Order Sauropterygia: extinct plesiosaurs and relatives.
    Order Placodontia: extinct marine mollusc-eaters.
Subclass Ichthyopterygia
    Order Ichthyosauria: extinct marine ichthyosaurs.

CHAPTER TWO

THE REPTILE BODY:
MORPHOLOGY AND FUNCTION

2.1 General body form

The stem reptiles or ancient Cotylosauria (Figure 1.1), compared with labyrinthodont amphibians, did not have any major modification in the supporting skeleton. They were heavy-limbed reptiles with a sprawling gait. The gait of chelonians is reminiscent of their Palaeozoic ancestors; for millions of years, chelonians retained the simple body form imposed upon them by their restricting shell. The general chelonian morphology restricts gait and speed of movement in terrestrial forms, but the width of the body and the short legs provide good stability. Locomotion in most species consists of a lateral sequence of leg movement, and a diagonal couplet walk, and a few species can shift from a walk to a walking trot. The body form, though simple, shows an interesting range amongst the Chelonia. For example, the Galapagos giant tortoise (*Geochelone elephantopus*) and other insular species are huge and have a high domed carapace. The recently extinct tortoise *Geochelone vosmaeri* (found until about 1800 on Rodrigues in the south-west Indian Ocean) had a shell raised at the front, enabling this species to browse and graze. Many amphibious terrapins are relatively small; others, such as the alligator snapping turtle (*Macroclemys temmincki*) are larger—up to 75 cm in length. Most modern chelonians have a long flexible neck which can be withdrawn: in the suborder Pleurodira the neck is retracted sideways and in the suborder Cryptodira the neck is retracted in an S-shaped vertical loop. Several divergent turtle families have evolved specializations of the plastron, permitting one or both ends of the shell to be closed.

Crocodilians are generally conservative in their body form, apart from the relative size and shape of the snout. Alligators and caimans (subfamily

Alligatorinae) have broad rounded snouts, the snout of the gharial or
gavial (subfamily Gavialinae) is long and slender, and there is tremendous
variation in the shape of the snout of the crocodile (subfamily
Crocodylinae). Crocodilians have at least three terrestrial gaits: the high
walk, the gallop and the belly run. The body is raised above the ground
during the high walk and the gallop but in the belly run (a rapid escape
reaction) the belly touches the ground, lizard-fashion.

The one surviving species of the order Rhynchocephalia is also
conservative in form, and retains many primitive and unique features:
amphicoelous vertebrae (concave at each end), well-developed median eye,
and teeth present on the jaws and on the outer margins of the palatines.

It is amongst the three suborders of the Squamata that we find a most
interesting range of adaptive modifications in general body form. The
amphisbaenians, lizards and snakes have a modified diapsid skull and
there is a wide range of adaptive modifications in the limbs, with a trend
towards limb reduction. The "worm-like" amphisbaenians with their scales

---

Figure 2.1   Form and function in the family Scincidae.
Subfamily Scincinae:
(a) *Eumeces fasciatus*, five-lined skink, eastern North America. Snout-vent length (s-v), 7 cm.
Agile with strong limbs and toes. The genus includes forms adapted to diverse habitat.
(b) *Scincus scincus*, common skink, Senegal, Egypt and Israel. Up to about 21 cm, sturdy
cylindrical body, tip of snout wedge-shaped. Short legs bear five toes with serrated edges. Able
to move rapidly in sand.
(c) *Ophiomorus punctatissimus*, speckled sand skink. Greece and Asia Minor. Limbs
completely absent. Popularly called sand skinks, up to about 20 cm with wedge-shaped snout.
(d) *Chalcides chalcides*, western Mediterranean. Total length up to 42 cm. Three toes on
limbs. During rapid movement, legs pressed against cylindrical body.
Subfamily Lygosominae:
(e) *Leiolopisma guichenoti*, s-v length about 4 cm. Southeastern Australia, diurnal and one of
the most abundant species.
(f) *Sphenomorphus kosciuskoi*, s-v length about 8 cm, disjunct distribution in montane areas
of Eastern Australia where it inhabits montane scrub vegetation. Particularly agile.
(g) *Pseudemoia spenceri*, about 5 cm s-v length. Somewhat dorso-ventrally flattened and well
adapted to using rocky exfoliations.
(h) *Mabuya sulcata*, a southwest African lizard with fully developed limbs and reaching up to
about 11 cm s-v length. Found above ground in sandy areas where there are trees and rocky
outcrops.
(i) *Ctenotus saxatilis*, 8 cm s-v length. Found in Central Australia where it inhabits rock
outcrops. The genus includes many sympatric species.
Subfamily Tiliquinae:
(j) *Tiliqua scincoides*, the popular "blue-tongued lizard" about 30 cm s-v length. Diurnal
slow moving lizard found in wide variety of habitats. Limbs short and body robust, smooth
scales.
(k) *Egernia saxatilis*, 13 cm s-v length, scales rough and multicarinate. Well adapted for living
in and amongst rocks and rocky crevices. Drawings by S. M. House.

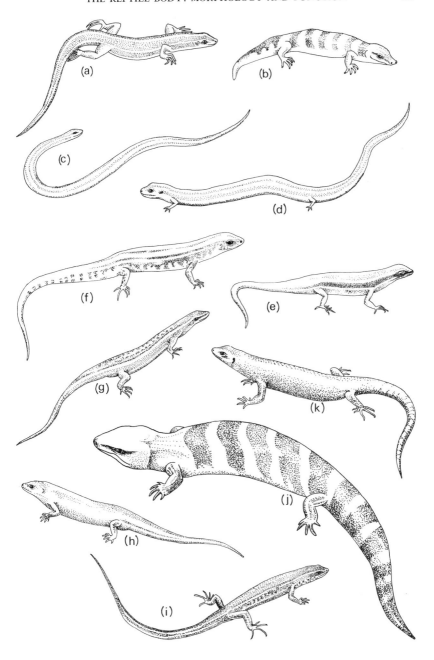

Table 2.1 Extent of diversity in the family Colubridae

Subfamily*	Distribution	Examples of specialized features
Xenodermatinae	Southern and southeastern Asia	Body scales reduced and separated and show a gradation between the unique acrochordid condition of non-overlapping, widely separated granules and the typical colubrine condition with overlapping ventral scales (gastrosteges). Lip scales with rear edges curved to various degrees. Mainly nocturnal. For example *Xenodermus* is found in the wet and humid rice fields of Java and feeds on frogs.
Pareinae and Dipsadinae	Former is Asian and latter is American	The two subfamilies include about 75 species; most are nocturnal with large eyes. Many are arboreal with long slender bodies and proportionally long tails. They seem to feed mainly on molluscs. Teeth are not present on the anterior part of the maxillary. When feeding, the lower jaw is thrust forward into the opening of the shell, soft tissue is hooked out by the snake's mandibular teeth. The snout is blunt and bones of the upper jaw and palate are not connected to the quadrates. Examples include *Dipsas* and *Sibon*.
Dasypeltinae	Ethiopian (some include Oriental species)	These are the "true" egg-eating snakes (*Dasypeltis*) which feed entirely on hard-shelled eggs. Most have a small head and a long slender body. The neck and mouth is flexible. Teeth reduced in size and number with a few at the rear of the upper jaw. Lower jaw very long, hinging well behind the end of the cranium. After the egg is engulfed, the shell is broken by combined action of the neck muscles and elongated vertebral processes. The egg contents are squeezed into the stomach and the crushed shell is regurgitated.
Homalopsinae	Indo-Australian	Robust bodies, short tails and completely aquatic, found in fresh water and in marine tidal zone. They are venomous and feed on fish and amphibians. Adaptations include small eyes directed upwards, crescentric nostrils on upper surface of head which can be closed. Maxillary teeth increase in size towards the posterior where there is a diastema followed by enlarged grooved teeth. Examples include *Homalopsis* and *Erpeton*.

Colubrinae	Cosmopolitan	Largest and most diverse family, relatively unspecialized, ventral scales on most forms well developed. The following genera give an indication of the range in form. *Coluber* (racers). Europe, Asia, northern Africa, North and Central America. Medium to large-sized, slender with a distinct head and long tail. Oviparous. Terrestrial but good climbers. *Coronella* (smooth snakes). Europe and Asia. Small to medium size. Scales lack keels. Prey on other reptiles and also small mammals. *Diadophis* (ringneck snakes). Small, semi-fossorial, insectivorous. North America. *Dispholidus* (boomslang). Ethiopian. Arboreal and diurnal, feeding mainly on birds, eggs, and chamaeleons. Highly venomous, grooved teeth are placed further forward than in most colubrids. *Eirenis* (dwarf snakes). Caucasus and Asia Minor. Small and mainly insectivorous. *Elaphe* (rat snakes). Distributed in both Old and New World. Large and terrestrial, semi-arboreal, carnivorous, feeding mainly on small rodents. *Lampropeltis* (king snakes). Southern North America and Central America. Medium size, small head, short tail and smooth scales. Terrestrial, diet includes other reptiles and small mammals. Closely related to the smooth snakes.
Natricinae	Cosmopolitan	Together with the Colubridinae they make up more than half of the world's snakes. They are almost exclusively aquatic or terrestrial. Teeth are fairly uniform and the iris is simple. Two best-known genera are *Natrix* and *Thamnophis*.
Aparallactinae	Africa and Middle East	Sometimes included with the vipers, these are the mole vipers (*Atractaspis*) and their allies. Small, blunt snout, small eyes, cylindrical body and short tail. All have well-developed venom apparatus, tooth rows much reduced but fangs relatively large. They are strongly fossorial.

* Classification follows that of Parker, H. W. (1965), 2nd Edition by Grandison, A. G. C. (1977).

arranged in rings have no limbs (except in the case of the Mexican *Bipes* which has short forelimbs) and the limb girdles are vestigial.

The lizards embrace at least 19 families and have a wide geographical distribution. Their diverse ecology is reflected in a range of body size; from the small, delicate, insectivorous night lizards (family Xantusiidae) to the large predatory monitor lizards (family Varanidae). In the Scincidae, one family of lizards which appear to be conservative in body form, there are terrestrial, arboreal, burrowing and aquatic forms. The variety of body form found in the Scincidae, and an indication of their diverse and specialized ecology, are shown in Figure 2.1.

Limbs are the principal means of locomotion in most lizards. There is, however, a considerable range in the rate at which different species can run. Notable is the rapid bipedal locomotion of some agamids and iguanids. Some arboreal lizards (e.g. the flying lizard, *Draco*, an agamid from Malaya), are adept at gliding, and have an expansion of skin (patagia) supported by ribs. Of the many lizard species with well-developed limbs, some have specially modified digits used for climbing. Chameleons, for example, have digits permanently opposed in groups of two and three, so as to grasp twigs and branches. Most of the geckos have toes which are broad or expanded at the tips, on which there are lamellae (flaps of skin) arranged in a transverse or fanwise fashion. In climbing, suction is not used, but numerous microscopic hooks in the lamellae catch in the irregularities of the surfaces being climbed.

The suborder Ophidia (Serpentes), with 11 families, have no limbs or limb girdles, except in the more primitive forms where there are vestigial hind limbs and pelvic girdles (Boidae) or rudiments of the pelvic girdle (Typhlopidae, or blind snakes). Although similar in basic body form, the snakes show adaptive radiation—there are burrowing, swimming, terrestrial and arboreal species. An indication of the extent of adaptive radiation in one family, the Colubridae, is shown in Table 2.1.

All species of limbless tetrapods, including snakes, make use of lateral undulatory locomotion (Gans, 1962). When a snake moves in this way, its body makes a series of lateral or horizontal waves. Forward movement is possible as each curve of the body thrusts against the rough ground surface. Rectilinear locomotion in snakes (and in amphisbaenians) consists of concertina-like movements: parts of the snake's body in turn bend, stretch and rebend, the weight and friction of the coiled part of the snake's body providing an effective basis (Bellairs, 1969). A particularly interesting and effective form of locomotion, and one unique to snakes, is sidewinding. This consists of movements at an acute angle, backwards along the longitudinal axis of the body. Section by section the snake's body is shifted from one axis to a near-parallel axis. Sidewinding is typically used by snakes in the family Viperidae and the step-like movement is potentially more rapid than the rectilinear movement.

2.2 Tails and tail autotomy

Reptile tails have a considerable variety of form and function. Their tails can be used in climbing, for social signals, in sexual displays, in territorial defence (Chapter 7), and for storage of fat.

Tail autotomy (self-mutilation) is the ability to shed the tail voluntarily. This evolved at an early stage in the evolution of reptiles and is essentially a

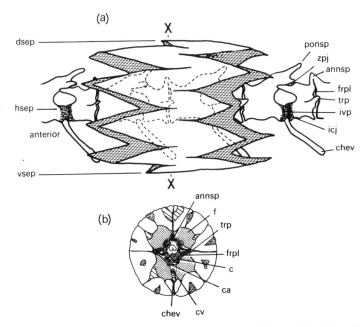

Figure 2.2 Tail autotomy in the lizard *Lacerta vivipara*. (*a*) relationships of muscles and vertebrae in mid-caudal region. Muscles of a single autotomy segment are shown. (*b*) transverse section (XX) through middle of tail in region of the autotomy plane. annsp, anterior neural spine. c, centrum. ca, caudal artery. cv, caudal vein. chev, chevron bone. dsep, dorsal part of median longitudinal septum. f, fat band. frpl, vertebral fracture plane. hsep, horizontal longitudinal septum. icj, intercentral joint. ivp, cartilaginous intervertebral pad. ponsp, posterior neural spine. trp, transverse process. vsep, ventral part of median longitudinal septum. zpj, zygapophysial joint. Redrawn from Sheppard, L. and Bellairs, A. d'A. (1972) *Brit. J. Herpetol.*, **4**, 276–286.

form of escape behaviour, either directing the predator to the writhing, detached tail, or enabling the reptile to break free if it is caught by the tail, or both. The process of tail autotomy involves muscular contraction and in most cases the fracture occurs through a caudal vertebra and not between the vertebrae (Figure 2.2). A fracture or autotomy plane exists in the caudal vertebrae of *Sphenodon*, a few snake species (e.g. *Pliocercus*), and in many lizard species (Simpson, 1965). In some gekkonid lizards it has been found that the incidence of tail autotomy is related to body temperature (Bustard, 1968), being high at 4°C (large portion of the tail shed), low or absent at 11°C, but again high at 19°C–29°C (small portion of the tail shed). It is interesting to consider the reason for this, but of greater importance is the overall value and adaptive strategies for tail autotomy. In 1977 Vitt *et al.* published an account of adaptive strategies and energetics of tail autotomy in four species of lizards. It was found that in some species where tail autotomy is most important for escape, regenerated tails are at least as large as the original tails. Species with alternative uses for the tail (sexual displays, balance, climbing) allocated less energy to regeneration, and the regenerated tails had a lower energy content.

2.3   Integument

The reptile skin has two main layers, an epidermis derived from ecto-dermal tissue and a dermis derived from mesodermal tissue. The epidermis has at least 6–8 cell layers. The reptile skin must be kept in good condition, and there is a continual replacement of damaged cells. To this end all reptiles periodically shed the superficial epidermal layers either as pieces, or as complete sloughs (Maderson, 1965). The frequency of skin shedding or sloughing is influenced in part by temperature, the age of the reptile, and its rate of ingestion. The shed skin represents an energy loss to the animal, the value of which can be expressed as part of the energy budget for that species. Smith (1976), for example, calculated energy budgets for two snake species maintained in the laboratory at 25°C. In the block diagram (Figure 2.3) the energy lost to sloughing can be compared with other energy costs; for the snake *Elaphe guttata*, 3% of the energy derived from initial ingestion is lost to sloughing, and for *Heterodon platyrhinos* the loss is 11%.

Scales are an obvious characteristic of reptiles, and in many species the pattern and number of scales are important features used in classification. The reptile scale has a complex histology. It is derived from the epidermis, but is not homologous with the dermal scales of fish. Although reptile

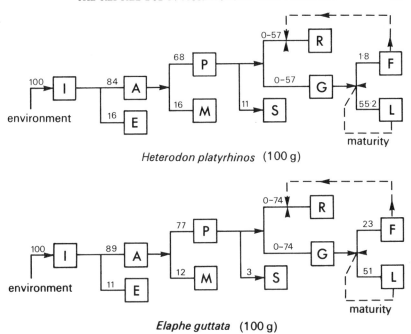

Figure 2.3 Sloughing energy requirements in two species of snake maintained at 25°C. All values expressed as percent of initial ingestion. I = ingested energy; A = assimilated energy; E = unassimilated energy; P = production of tissue; M = metabolic cost; S = sloughing cost; R = reproduction; G = growth; F = fat accumulations; L = lean-dry biomass. Redrawn from Smith, G. C. (1976) *Ecology*, **57**, 252–264.

scales may appear to be separate structures, they are in fact localized thickenings of a continuous sheet of tissue. Interesting work by Dhouailly (1975) has shown remarkable similarity in the mechanisms of skin differentiation of reptiles and birds. It was found that reptilian epidermis, when confronted with reptilian or avian dermis, always responds to dermal messages by forming scale buds. This suggests that there is a very close relationship between morphogenesis of scales and feathers.

In some reptiles, epidermal scales are supported internally by a secondary mesodermal development, dermal scale or osteoderm—for example, the bony plates on the back and tail of the extinct stegosaurs were of this nature. All living crocodilians possess dermal scales and they are also found on the head in some lizards. In the Chelonia, the shell (carapace above, plastron below) has an epidermal horny surface cover, with a dermal bony armour beneath, and the pattern of dermal plates does not conform to the pattern and number of horny laminae.

There is considerable variety of size and texture of cutaneous scales amongst reptile groups, ranging from the overlapping tile-like scales of the Crocodilia to the typically granular scales of the Gekkonidiae. Locomotion in the limbless Squamata is basically by lateral undulation of the body. Many terrestrial snakes, however, also obtain assistance in locomotion from enlarged ventral scutes (gastrosteges), arranged in a single longitudinal row, and which have muscles inserted at their outer ends.

Are scales simply a by-product of a dry integument or is the variety of scale form indicative of particular functions? Obviously scale characteristics contribute to the general appearance of the reptile, and therefore scale texture, size, and colour can be linked to functional roles in social behaviour, camouflage, defence, and thermal relations. Based partly on an observation that in several genera of modern lizards scales are elongated in those forms found in warm climates, Regal (1975) has proposed that during evolution and radiation, there was an elongation of reptile body scales as an adaptive response to excessive solar heat; feathers may likewise have arisen as adaptations to intense solar radiation. It is certainly true that several authors have noted a correlation between reptile scale size and temperature regime: there are, for example, geographic clines in scale size of the South American iguanid *Liolaemus* which suggests that small scales are selectively advantageous in cool environments.

The reptile dermis consists of a thick connective tissue layer containing nerve tissue, blood vessels and pigment cells. It is mostly in the outer regions of the dermis that the chromatophores are found. The melanophore cells form the basis of dark coloration; other chromatophores in the dermis, such as lipophores, give a yellow or green appearance to the skin. Many reptiles have physiologically active melanophores which can lighten or darken the skin. The melanophores of chamaeleons seem to be controlled by the autonomic nervous system but in other groups there is both a hormonal and neural basis for colour change.

2.4 Skeleton and muscles

The reptile skull has been an object of much study, and we cannot do justice here to the vast body of knowledge that exists on this part of the skeleton. Characteristic is the single occipital condyle and the various modifications to the temporal region (Chapter 1). Romer (1956) has identified important evolutionary modifications in the reptile skull: 1, reduction, fusion, modification, or increase in individual dermal elements; 2, changes in skull proportions; 3, changes in skull openings; 4, changes in the temporal regions associated with the action of the temporal muscles; 5, modification of the palate; 6, variations in the occipital region; 7, variations in the ossification of the cranium.

In chelonians and crocodilians, the upper jaw is firmly attached to the base of the skull, whereas in the majority of lizards and snakes, there is cranial kinesis or independent movement—in typical snakes, the upper jaw is only loosely attached to the cranium. This condition imparts important advantages for aligning the upper and lower teeth when gripping prey and when moving the prey to the back of the mouth. In snakes, the form and function of the skull is both beautiful and spectacular (Figure 2.4). The maxillary arch is considerably modified and the symphysis between the halves of the lower jaw, while weak in many lizards, is absent in snakes, thus allowing extraordinarily large prey to be taken.

Crocodiles are large amphibious predators which seize and manipulate prey, and some characteristics of the skull have a recognizable functional role related to their feeding behaviour (Iordansky, 1973). For example, the elongated and often narrow jaws facilitate the capture of relatively small and agile prey such as fish. The inclined position of the quadrates, which displaces the jaw joint far posteriorly, increases the relative displacement of the tips of the jaw for a given angular opening. The undulation of the jaw margins (Figure 2.4) and the pseudoheterodonty allow the crocodile to hold prey firmly between the jaws. The longitudinal crests of the osteodermic relief may increase the mechanical strength of the flattened skull, and Iordansky also suggests that crests on the anteroventral surface of the quadrate to which the tendons and aponeuroses of the jaw adductors are attached, is a structural adaptation.

Reptiles have modified cervical vertebrae with an atlas and axis, but further specialization of the vertebra is minimal compared with mammals. In the primitive forms the vertebral centra are amphicoelous, but in most living forms they are procoelous (concave in front and convex behind). Each vertebra has a pair of zygapophyses on the front and rear of the neural arch, typical of some amphibians and the higher tetrapods (Figure 2.5). This form of articulation allows flexibility and strength in animals whose locomotion depends on distinct body movements. An interesting type of articulation is found in the Lepidosauria—in some (particularly snakes), the neural arch has two supplementary facets. These articular surfaces are opposite to the prezygapophyses and the surfaces form a tenon (zygosphene) set into a mortise (zygantrum) in the posterior face of the

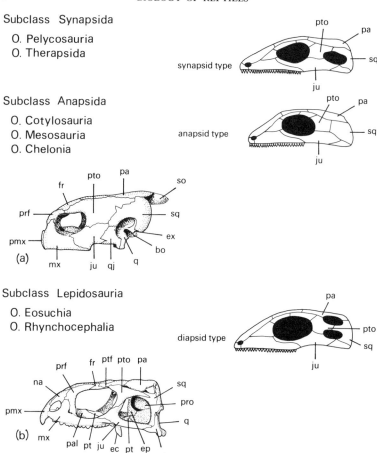

Subclass Synapsida

  O. Pelycosauria
  O. Therapsida

Subclass Anapsida

  O. Cotylosauria
  O. Mesosauria
  O. Chelonia

Subclass Lepidosauria

  O. Eosuchia
  O. Rhynchocephalia

Figure 2.4 Reptile skulls (drawn to different scales). (*a*) turtle (*Chelonia*); (*b*) tuatara (*Sphenodon*); (*c*) lizard (*Cyclura*); (*d*) amphisbaenian (*Amphisbaena fuliginosa*); (*e*) snake (*Ptyas*); (*f*) crocodile (*Osteolaemus*). ang, angular. bo, basioccipital. bs, basisphenoid. d, dentary. ec, ectopterygoid. ep, epipterygoid. ex, exoccipital. fr, frontal. is, interorbital septum. ju, jugal. la, lachrymal. mx, maxilla. na, nasal. pa, parietal. pal, palatine. palp, palpebral. pmx, premaxilla. prf, prefrontal. pro, prootic. ps, parasphenoid. pt, pterygoid. ptf, postfrontal. pto, postorbital. q, quadrate. qj, quadratojugal. smx, septomaxilla. so, supraoccipital. sq, squamosal. sta, stapes. su, supratemporal. sur, surangular. vo, vomer. (*a*), (*b*), (*c*) and (*e*) redrawn from Parker, H. W. (1977) *Snakes, A Natural History*, revised by Grandison, A. C. C., Cornell University Press. (*d*) redrawn from Zangerl, R. (1944) *Am. Mid. Nat.*, 31, 417–454. (*f*) redrawn from Bellairs (1969). Reptilian skull types redrawn from Romer, A. S. and Parsons, T. S. (1977) and Romer, A. S. (1956) *Osteology of the Reptiles*, Univ. of Chicago Press.

O. Squamata

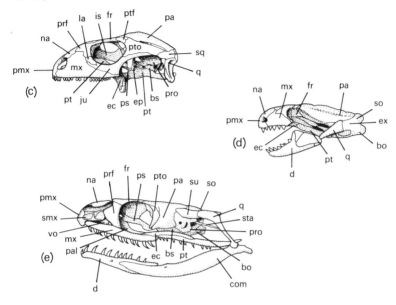

Subclass Archosauria

O. Thecodontia
O. Crocodilia

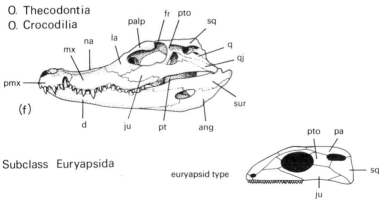

Subclass Euryapsida

Subclass Ichthyopterygia

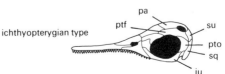

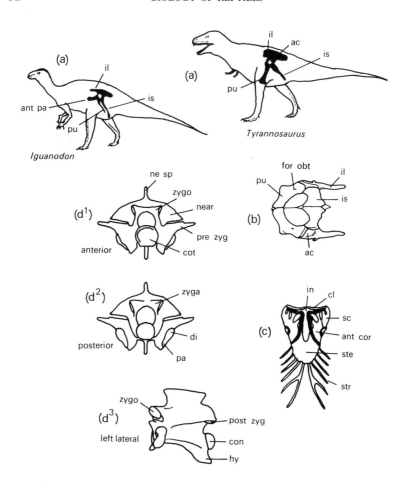

Figure 2.5   Reptile vertebrae and girdles (drawn to different scales). (*a*) tetraradiate pelvis of a bipedal ornithischian (*Iguanodon*) and triradiate pelvis of a bipedal Saurischian (*Tyrannosaurus*); (*b*) pelvic girdle of *Varanus* from below; (*c*) pectoral girdle of *Iguana* from below; (*d*) general morphological feature of trunk vertebrae of *Natrix*. ac, acetabulum. ant cor, anterior coracoid element. ant pu, anterior pubis. cl, clavicle. con, condyle. cot, cotyle. di, diapophysis. for obt, foramen for obturator nerve. hy, hypopophysis. il, ilium. in, interclavicle. is, ischium. near, neural arch. nesp, neural spine. pa, parapophysis. post zyg, post zygapophysis. pre zyg, prezygapophysial process. pu, pubis. sc, scapula. ste, sternum. str, sternal ribs. zyga, zygantrum. zygo, zygosphene. (*a*) based on British Museum Publication *Dinosaurs and their Living Relatives*; (*b*) redrawn from Bellairs, A. d'A. (1969) *The Life of Reptiles*; (*c*) redrawn from Romer, A. S. and Parsons, T. S. (1977); (*d*) redrawn from Hoffstetter, R. and Gasc, J.-P. (1969) in Gans, C. *et al.*, *Biology of the Reptilia*, Vol. 1, Academic Press, pp. 201–310.

neural arch of the preceding vertebra (Figure 2.5). Modern reptiles with well-developed limbs have two sacral vertebra which connect to fused expanded ribs attached to the ilium and provide support for the pelvis. The ribs occur on the pre-caudal vertebra and there is considerable variety of rib shape and attachment. Ribs of turtles are double-headed, and in the trunk region they are expanded so as to assist in the support of the carapace. The ribs of gliding reptiles such as *Draco* are particularly specialized in that the flaps of skin used in gliding are supported by elongated trunk ribs. Turtles and snakes do not have a sternum.

Girdles and limbs are basically similar to those found in amphibians. The pectoral girdle consists of a scapula, coracoid and procoracoid attached by muscle to the vertebral column. The humerus articulates at the junction of the scapula and coracoid. A space, the obturator foramen, is surrounded by the pubic symphysis and ischial symphysis (Figure 2.5). In the forms where limbs are the main means of locomotion, the humerus and femur are held so that the distal end is higher than the proximal, an arrangement known as abduction. The radius and ulna, and the tibia and fibula, are at right angles to the proximal limb bones and the feet are turned outwards in the typical reptilian stance.

Some evolutionary trends in the adaptive nature of reptile muscular systems will be noted here, but space does not permit more than an introduction to this complex topic. In general, and compared with amphibians, we find functional changes in reptile jaw musculature, and modification of body muscles to support the weight of the body. Development of openings (fenestrae) in the dermal covering of the cheek provided a better attachment for large muscle systems. Although the jaw muscular patterns of the lizards and snakes have many specialized features, some indication of the basic pattern for superficial muscles can be seen in the examples provided (Figure 2.6). The adductor mandibulae group, which runs from the dermal cranial elements and the quadrate to the lower jaw, provides the main jaw closing mechanism.

As in other tetrapods, two body muscles, the serratus ventralis (ventrally) and levator scapulae (dorsally) run from the scapulae and support the body in the pectoral region. The crest on the upper end of the humerus is for the insertion of the deltoideus and pectoralis muscles which originate from the pectoral girdle and sternum. These, together with the latissimus dorsi, inserted on the posterior side of the humerus, and the deeper subcoracoscapularis (Figure 2.6), help to raise, lower and manoeuvre the forelimb. Muscles of the limbs consist of dorsal extensors and ventral flexors as can readily be seen in the muscles of the hindlimbs and pelvic girdle of lizards and *Sphenodon*. The iliofemoralis and puboischiofemoralis internus (Figure 2.6) are on the dorsal surface and keep the femur raised. The deep muscles, such as the puboischiofemoralis externus and adductor femoris, originate on the pelvis and insert on the femur, and function to lower the femur and also flex the knee joint. Several superficial muscles on the ventral surface of the thigh act as flexors of the lower leg, and muscles which originate on the ventral side of the proximal caudal vertebrae and insert on the femur have an important role in forward movement. Hindlimbs of reptiles are generally larger with a more powerful muscular system than those of the forelimbs. Surprisingly, however, the anatomy of those lizards which have bipedal locomotion differs only slightly from forms which always walk on four legs. Snyder (1962) has noted that in iguanids there is a tendency for the length of the trunk to be reduced in the more accomplished bipedal lizards and for the disparity in length of the fore- and hindlimbs to increase. A change seen in the bipedal forms is the upward migration of parts of the limb muscles towards the body so that the distal parts of the limbs are in comparison slender and light.

2.5   Teeth and dentition

Apart from one extinct species, no adult Chelonia possess teeth, but some embryos have a partial dental lamina which disappears early in ontogeny. The shape of the beak and the presence of tooth-like serrations or cutting edges (tomia) on the beaks of some Chelonia is of interest and requires further research. All other reptiles have teeth and these are usually replaced

---

Figure 2.6   Reptile jaw superficial musculature and limb musculature (drawn to different scales). (*a*) lateral view of jaw muscles of an advanced colubrid snake; (*b*) lateral view of head of *Agama stellio* showing superficial muscles; (*c*) shoulder and upper arm muscles of a lizard; (*d*) limb muscles of the pelvis and thigh of a lizard. adf, adductor femoris. am, ambiens. bi, biceps. br, brachialis. cld, clavicular deltoid. cor, coracobrachialis. flte, flexor tibialis externus. flti, flexor tibialis internus. ilf, ileofemoralis. ilt, iliotibialis. latd, latissimus dorsi. lig, ligament caudifemorales. maesp, adductor mandibulae externus. mamem, adductor mandibulae externus medialis. mamep, adductor mandibulae externus profundus. mames, adductor mandibulae externus superficialis. mdm, depressor mandibulae. mdma, depressor mandibulae, accessory head. mimdp, intermandibularis posterior. mlao, levator anguli oris. mpt, pterygoideus. pe, pectoralis. pubfe, puboischiofemoralis externus. pubfi, puboischiofemoralis internus. pubo, pubotibialis. puboi, puboischiotibialis. qml, quadrato-maxillary ligament. scd, scapular deltoid. sch, scapulohumeralis anterior. sub sc, subcoraco-scapularis. supr, supracoracoideus. tm, tympanic membrane. tri, triceps. (*a*) and (*b*) redrawn from Haas, G. (1973) in Gans, C., *Biology of the Reptilia*, Vol. 4, Academic Press, pp. 285–490. (*c*) and (*d*) redrawn from Romer and Parsons (1977).

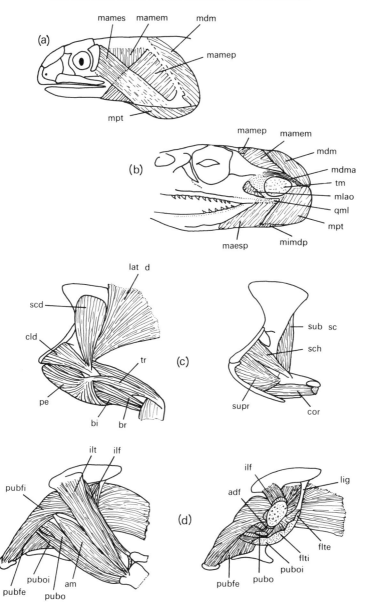

continuously; in *Sphenodon* and agamids, however, the teeth are probably not replaced in adults, and are usually badly worn. As in other tetrapods the tooth has hard dentine tissue sometimes capped with "enamel".

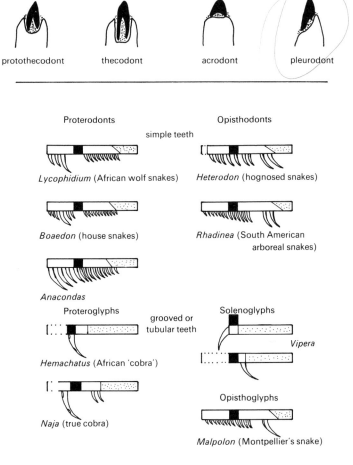

Figure 2.7 Reptile dentition. Above, common types of implantation. Below, schematic diagrams showing arrangement of maxillary teeth in snakes. In the proterodonts there is an increasing reduction of simple posterior teeth. In the opisthodonts there is suppression of simple anterior teeth. Venomous snakes fall into three categories, proteroglyphs and solenoglyphs (both with fangs in front of the upper jaw) and the opisthoglyphs (grooved teeth on the back of the upper jaw). The black square on the maxilla is the zone of the maxillofrontal support. Redrawn from Edmund, A. G. (1969) in Gans, C. *et al.*, *Biology of the Reptilia*, Vol. 1, Academic Press, pp. 117–200.

Modern Crocodilia have pseudoheterodent dentition, that is, the teeth are uniform and conical in shape, but the height and thickness of the teeth in the upper jaw increases, starting from anteriormost, then decreases gradually only to increase again. Also, the teeth occur only on jawbones, and in sockets (thecodont) as in mammals. In alligators, the fourth tooth in the lower jaw fits into a laterally closed pit in the upper jaw, while the fourth tooth on the upper jaw is well developed. In crocodiles the fourth tooth of the lower jaw fits into a notch in the upper jaw but the tooth is visible when the jaw is closed, and the largest tooth of the upper jaw is the fifth. Most lizards have a pleurodont dentition (teeth attached obliquely to the jaw edge, Figure 2.7) and some have additional teeth on the palatine and pterygoid bones. Few species have specialized teeth or heterodont dentition (different sized or shaped specialized teeth); one example is the lower teeth of the lizard *Heloderma*, which have grooves down which poison can pass from the venom glands.

The teeth of snakes are probably best known for their fang-like appearance (Figure 2.7). Snakes have a pleurodont dentition—the teeth are sharp and re-curved, and in venomous snakes are grooved or tubular for injection of venom. The back-fanged snakes have grooved teeth attached to the back of the upper jaw (opisthoglyphous), whereas other forms (elapids and hydrophids) have grooved or elongated hollow teeth attached to the maxillary bone in front of the upper jaw (proteroglyphous). Vipers have large, tubular, retractable fangs (solenoglyphous). A few species such as the egg-eating snakes (*Dasypeltis*) have teeth which are reduced in size and in number. The teeth of most snakes are highly suitable for piercing and grasping, but not for dealing with hard-bodied prey, although Savitzky (1981) recently reported a previously unrecognized durophagic adaptation in snakes: hinged teeth that enable snakes to grasp and to swallow hard-bodied prey.

2.6 Diet

Chelonians are in general omnivorous although some are selective feeders and could be considered as strictly carnivorous. For example, the loggerhead turtle (*Caretta caretta*) feeds on crabs and other crustaceans, molluscs, fish and only occasionally on algae. The single representative of the order Rhynchocephalia (*Sphenodon*) is strictly carnivorous, consuming a wide variety of prey ranging from arthropods to small birds and mammals.

The lizards as a group are primarily insectivorous, although some feed on larger animals and some on carrion. An arthropod diet, principally of insects, has been recorded for a large number of lizard species, but some age-specific shifts in diet from principally insectivorous to herbivorous have also been noted. A small number of species are herbivorous, for example *Tiliqua* and *Amblyrhynchus*. These herbivorous species nearly always exceed 100 g in body weight. Many ideas have been put forward to account for differences in diet and body weight. Recent accounts suggest that lizards have difficulty utilizing plant material because of an inability to chew properly, and what appears to be a lack of microbial populations to assist digestion of the cellulose. However, Nagy (1977) found that in the case of the strictly herbivorous *Sauromalus obesus*, cellulose activity in the intestine was similar to that in a cow's rumen but that cellulose digestion was not of major importance in the energy balance of this species. In a later study of the digestive efficiency of the small omnivorous xantusiid lizard *Klauberina riversiana*, Johnson and Lillywhite (1979) found only a small difference between digestive efficiencies of those *Klauberina* fed on apple and those fed on mealworms. Based on morphological characters, *Klauberina* (small compared to most herbivorous lizards) appears to be basically insectivorous, but clearly small lizards such as this species also have the ability to utilize and digest vegetation.

There are many good accounts of the type and amount of food consumed by different lizard species and it is clear from these that there are many interesting differences in the size of prey selected. Males and females of the same species may select prey of different sizes because the male is larger and has a larger jaw. Interspecific differences in prey size selection are also known and this may in part act to reduce competition for food.

Although most snakes are carnivorous, a few fossorial forms are insectivorous. Apart from research on the specialized diets of egg-eating snakes (Dasypeltinae) there are few accounts of selective predation by snakes and very little analysis of the energetics of snake feeding ecology. Rather than being opportunistic in their feeding habits, some species according to recent evidence optimize their foraging so as to obtain most gain for least effort. Some viperine snakes (*Natrix maura*, for example) select the size of their prey (fish) with the result that the balance between effort and return is optimized (Davies *et al.*, 1980). A good general account of ecological applications of cost-benefit analysis to predator-prey inter-actions has been written by Krebs and Davies (1978).

Ontogenetic shifts in prey preferences are well known for many species, and this change in diet has sometimes been attributed to maturation of prey handling ability. However, more recent research is beginning to show that the energetic requirements of snakes are an important aspect of prey selection, and that ontogenetic shifts in diet can only partly be attributed to handling ability. Typical of more recent and detailed analyses of snake foraging ecology is that by Godley (1980) who for several years studied the striped swamp snake *Regina alleni*. This species has dramatic seasonal and ontogenetic shifts in food habits, the ecological and energetic consequences of which can be interpreted in terms of the divergent life histories and growth patterns of the predator and its prey. Juvenile snakes took more but smaller prey than adults, feeding on odonate naiads that were higher in protein but lower in ash content than the decapods taken by the adults. The energetic intake per gram snake body mass was therefore generally higher in juveniles. This type of detailed analysis makes an important contribution to reptile ecology and is certain to give incentive for further important research.

Crocodilians are strictly carnivorous, feeding on prey ranging in size from arthropods to birds and mammals. Some species employ the tail to assist in prey capture; as has been described (Section 2.5) the crocodilian jaw is well modified to hold and to manoeuvre prey.

2.7   Digestive system

The action of the jaws, and to some extent tongue movements, enable reptiles to manoeuvre and swallow food. Compared with amphibians, the reptile tongue, particularly in the Squamata, shows considerable variation in both shape and structure. In lizards there is a protrusible fore-tongue and in some insectivorous forms (e.g. chamaeleons) this is used primarily for catching prey. Tongue flicking is well known in both lizards and snakes as part of the chemosensory system. In snakes the tongue is long, slender and deeply forked, and can be retracted into a sheath of tissue which passes back beneath the glottis, larynx and front part of the trachea.

Reptiles were the first major group to occupy dry land and this required (together with other changes) important evolutionary changes to the oral glands, especially for immobilizing prey (venom glands), and swallowing it (glands to provide lubricating secretions). It is not surprising therefore that the evolution of the oral glands (Figure 2.8) in reptiles has resulted in complex and specialized secretory systems. Duvernoy's gland has been found in many of the colubrids: in the highly venomous *Dispholidus typus* (boomslang) this gland is most elaborate. Although Duvernoy's gland may produce toxic secretions, the term "venom glands" is best applied in the strict sense to the glands of the Elapidae, Viperidae and *Atractaspis*

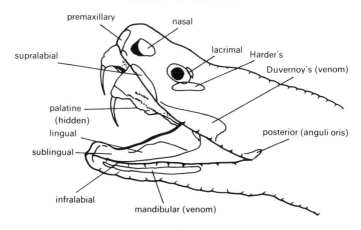

Figure 2.8 Location of the major glands of the head. Redrawn from Kochva, E. (1978) in Gans, C. and Gans, K. A., *Biology of the Reptilia*, Vol. 8, Academic Press, pp. 43–162.

(Kochva, 1978). The venom glands are structurally different in each group and probably had separate origins in the Elapidae and the Viperidae. Venom glands lie on the side of the head and neck; leading from them ducts extend along the labial sides of the maxilla to enter the region surrounding the base of the modified maxillary teeth (in the lizard *Heloderma* one of the dental glands produces venom). Snake venom, which contains complex enzymes and protein-like substances, is used to immo-bilize prey and also to assist digestion. It has two principal characteristics, one haemolytic and one neurotoxic. Generally, no one species has venom with a single characteristic, but one effect is usually more marked than the other. Venom of the Gila monster is primarily neurotoxic. A useful and detailed account of the rather complex subject of venoms and venomous animals is to be found in Bücherl *et al.* (1968).

The alimentary canal has basically the same design as in other higher vertebrates, with secretions from mucous cells and muscular walls assisting the movement of food from mouth to stomach. The oesophagus, although a simple tube, can be distinguished from the stomach, and its diameter can easily be increased to facilitate the passage of large prey items. Generally, the oesophagus of snakes has more folds than in other reptiles, and this possibly also facilitates the passage of very large prey. Specialized egg-eating snakes have anterior vertebral ventral hypapophyses which project through the oesophagus wall and these serve to break and crush the egg shell (Gans, 1952); in some turtles there are oesophageal spines which help to crush the food.

Digestion commences mainly in the stomach. Cells of the stomach wall secrete enzymes which, together with acid gastric juices, break down protein. The rate of digestion is dependent partly on body temperature (Chapter 5) so that below certain temperature levels putrefaction may predominate over digestion. The small intestine is coiled and is mainly concerned with absorption of food, and in all groups except Crocodilia, there is a short colic caecum at the junction of the small intestine and the wider large intestine. The large intestine, which in herbivorous forms has a greater volume than in insectivorous forms, passes on to a cloacal chamber. This chamber is subdivided into a coprodaeum for receiving faeces and a urodaeum for urine and products of the genital organs, and the common proctodaeum is closed by a cloacal sphincter. The cloaca has an important role in the reabsorption of water (Chapter 5). The liver and pancreas both have an important role in digestion—the liver excretes nitrogenous waste products and is generally very large and lobed, and the pancreas, an endocrine gland, has a synthetic ability which allows the gland to adapt the enzymatic composition of the pancreatic juice to the diet in different reptiles (Florkin and Scheer, 1974). Smooth muscles of the gastrointestinal tract help to mix digestive juices with the gut contents and also assist the movement of the contents. A measure of the effective action of the gut as a whole can be obtained from studies of the apparent digestibility coefficient (ADC) or apparent efficiency of assimilation. This is expressed by the percentage of the utilized portion of energetic values of the food, and values of ADC in general tend to be higher (70–98 %) for insectivorous and carnivorous species than for herbivorous forms which have an ADC of 30–56 % (Skoczylas, 1978).

Lipid reserves are stored subcutaneously or in visceral fat bodies (corpora adiposa). The storage, utilization, and cycling of lipid reserves (Figure 2.9) have been shown to have many important functions in reptiles: reproduction, maintenance during winter dormancy, and growth. For example, the seasonal cycling of lipids in tropical anoles (Figure 2.9) can be related to food availability. Tropical anoles live in regions where there is a wet and a dry season. Sufficient food is available to the adults during the dry season, and the energy that would have been put into reproduction at this time is conserved in the form of lipids. As a result, lipid levels increase during the dry season and this stored energy allows the anoles to produce a greater number of young during the following wet season. Snakes may utilize lipids during winter dormancy. The data for

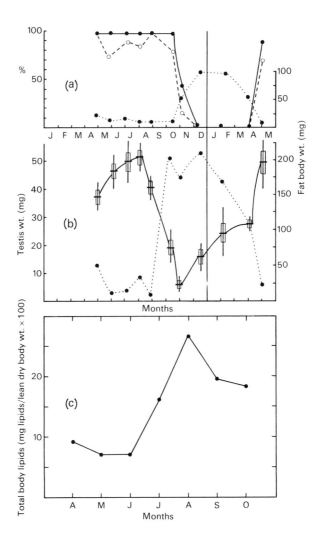

Figure 2.9 Graphs (a) and (b) are for reproductive and fat body cycles for *Anolis grahami*, from Licht, P. and Gorman, G. C. (1970) *Univ. Calif. Publ. Zool.*, **45**, 1–52. (a) depicts the percentage of females in reproductive condition (●——●) and weight of fat bodies (● ⋯ ●). (b) represents the same, only for males, and also contains the number of lizards examined (abscissa). (c) shows seasonal variation in total body lipids in *Thamnophis sirtalis parietalis* (from Aleksiuk, M. and Stewart, K. W. (1971) *Ecology*, **52**, 485–490). The wintering period extends from October to April and reproduction occurs from June to August.

Thamnophis sirtalis (Figure 2.9) show that before winter dormancy, lipid levels are typically increased; this increase seems to be important for maintenance during winter. Derickson (1976) has reviewed lipid storage and utilization in reptiles and concludes that in some cases a correlation exists between patterns of lipid cycling and life histories, with food availability being the ultimate determining factor.

2.8 Respiratory systems and blood systems

The lungs of *Sphenodon* are primitive and similar to those of anurans; lungs of snakes are also simple, often with a saclike end, and many have only a single functional lung, the right. Lizards, some turtles and crocodiles have lungs similar in appearance to those of mammals. The larynx with its skeletal support of paired arytenoid cartilages and incomplete cricoid ring is at the anterior part of the trachea. The trachea is supported by cartilages and within the thorax is divided into two bronchi. The lungs lie in a cavity (the pleuroperitoneal cavity) and the activity of the intercostal muscles via a backward-forward movement of the ribs is the main agent for inhalation and exhalation of air. Crocodilians have a transverse non-muscular partition (post-hepatic septum) separating the pleural cavity from the peritoneal cavity. This partition, which is continuous with a diaphragmatic muscle, may assist in respiration, but it is not homologous with the mammalian diaphragm. Chelonians change the size of their body cavity by contractions of the antagonistic muscles in the flank and shoulder region. Some aquatic turtles respire via the skin, pharynx and cloaca, as well as the lung.

The reptile heart, which compared to that of amphibians is shortened at both ends, has a partly divided single ventricle, except in crocodiles and alligators where there is a complete interventricular septum (Figure 2.10). There are two separate auricles, the right receiving deoxygenated blood, the left receiving oxygenated blood. In the non-crocodilian groups the main interventricular septum lies in a horizontal plane, thus tending to divide the ventricle into a dorsal and ventral chamber. The main anterior vessels include the pulmonary trunk, giving rise to the pulmonary arteries, and two systemic trunks: one leads to the right aorta and one to the left aorta (Figure 2.10). The pulmonary trunk branches from the ventral chamber, and the right systemic trunk from the dorsal ventricular chamber. The right aorta crosses over the left and leads to the right aortic arch, then dividing into the common carotid arteries. The left aorta receives its blood via an interventricular canal (in crocodiles via the

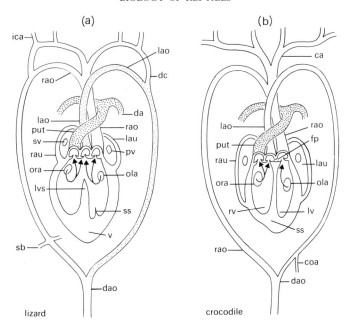

Figure 2.10   Diagram of a lizard heart (*a*) and a crocodile heart (*b*) with the great vessels in ventral view. Vessels carrying venous blood stippled, those carrying mixed blood stippled lightly. ca, carotid-subclavian stem (left side). coa, coeliac artery. da, ductus arteriosus. dao, dorsal aorta. dc, ductus coroticus. fp, foramen of Panizza. ica, internal carotid artery. ivs, main interventricular septum. lao, left aorta (systemic arch). lau, left auricle. lv, left ventricle. ola, opening of left auricle into ventricle. ora, opening of right auricle. put, pulmonary trunk. pv, opening of pulmonary vein into left auricle. rao, right aorta (systemic arch). rau, right auricle. rv, right ventricle. sb, subclavian artery. ss, secondary interventricular septum. sv, sinus venosus opening into right auricle. v, ventricle. Redrawn from Bellairs, A. (1969) after Hughes, G. M. (1965) *Comparative Physiology of Vertebrate Respiration*, Heinemann.

foramen of Panizza from the left ventricle). Essentially reptiles do have a double circulation, but it is not as physiologically efficient as in mammals and birds.

The erythrocytes of reptiles are generally oval, and are nucleated, Eosinophilic and basophilic granulocytes and thrombocytes are relatively homogeneous. The plasma is usually colourless or straw-coloured, but in some species contains pigments.

Lymphatic vessels are present in reptiles, and the lymphatic system, which is an additional means of returning fluid from the cells to the heart, resembles that found in salamanders. However, in most reptiles examined there is a pair of muscular contractile lymph "hearts" in the pelvic region and these are not found, or are not functional, in the higher tetrapods. The lymph nodes or aggregations of lymphoid tissue are sparsely represented. Lymphocytes are an important class of leucocytes and there is a considerable range in their size.

2.9   Urogenital system

The kidney of an adult reptile is a true metanephros (functional kidney) discharging by a single ureter. The pronephros is present and functional only during early embryonic development. During development, the mesonephric kidneys or Wolffian bodies become well developed and consist of large numbers of tubules. Later a metanephric kidney completely assumes the function of the mesonephros. Metanephric tubules lack nephrostomes and do not open into the peritoneal cavity. Glomeruli are present, but compared with those found in mammals, they tend to be small and few in number. It has been suggested that this is an adaptation which conserves water by reducing the flow of urine passed into the tubule. Terrestrial and freshwater turtles, and also lizards, generally have a urinary bladder, while in snakes the ureter dilates in the posterior region to form a small urinary reservoir. The urine of many Chelonia and the Crocodilia is fluid, while that voided by snakes, lizards and tortoises which inhabit arid regions, contains crystals of insoluble urates.

The ovaries are always paired and often large, probably because the egg contains a large quantity of yolk (a complex of proteins, phospholipids, and fats). The separate oviducts have independent funnel-shaped ostia, and are provided in some forms with glandular walls which secrete the albumen and the shell. Like the ovaries, the oviducts will, in many species, increase in size during the breeding season. The ova are contained in ovarian (Graafian) follicles in the walls of the ovaries; the number maturing at any one time is small compared with those found in many amphibians. Fertilization is always internal and takes place in the upper portion of the oviducts. Special sperm-storing glands occur at the base of the infundibulum of the oviduct of colubrid and viperid snakes, and tubules for sperm storage have been found in some turtles, *Anolis* (lizards) and in representatives of the Chamaeleontidae (Fox, 1963).

The elongated testes of reptiles are connected with an epididymis of mesonephric origin. In lizards and snakes the right testis is generally located anterior to the left and both are vascularized by spermatic arteries and veins; the Wolffian duct does not have an excretory function, but is a reproductive duct which transports sperm. Apart from *Sphenodon*, all living male reptiles possess some form of intromittent organ. In the Chelonia and Crocodilia this is a single structure, with a groove along the surface providing a passage for the sperm. Lizards and snakes have intromittent organs consisting of a pair of saclike structures called hemipenes, which, when relaxed, lie under the skin resulting in a thickening of the tail base. Hemipenes are tubular in structure and a longitudinal groove (sulcus spermaticus) on each provides a passage for the sperm. Only one is inserted during copulation. Each of the hemipenes is permeated with blood and lymph sinuses and after eversion and erection, structures previously lying on the inner surface are externally placed. There is considerable variety in the form and structure of the hemipenes, and interspecific differences are thought to be important reproductive isolating mechanisms in some species.

2.10   Nervous system and sense organs

As in other vertebrates, the reptile brain is organized on a basic plan of three divisions established in the embryo (Figure 2.11). The prosencephalon includes both the telencephalon (cerebral hemispheres including olfactory lobes, cerebral cortex, olfactory bulbs) and the diencephalon (epithalamus, dorsal thalamus, ventral thalamus and hypothalamus). The mesencephalon embraces the tectum including the optic lobes, and the tegmentum. The rhombencephalon includes the medulla oblongata and the cerebellum.

In the Lacertilia, Crocodilia and *Sphenodon*, a long peduncle extends anteriorly from each cerebral hemisphere, terminating in an olfactory bulb. The peduncle is shorter and thicker in snakes and in the lizard *Anguis fragilis*, but is practically absent in the Chelonia. Olfactory structures are well developed in the Chelonia and are proportionately shorter in other orders. Accessory bulbs (absent in Crocodilia and in small Chelonia) are present posterior to the main bulbs in the Squamata and in *Sphenodon*

Figure 2.11   Diagram showing the essential features of the reptile brain and reptile eye (seen in transverse section through the middle of the lens). ce, cerebellum. chi, chiasma. cho, chorioid plexus. cil, ciliary muscle. co, cornea. con, conus pupillaris. die, diencephalon. ep, epiphysis. ey, eyelid. har, Harderian gland. hy, hypophysis. ir, iris. le, lens. me, medulla oblongata. ol, olfactory bulb. opt, optic nerve. re, retina. sclc, scleral cartilage. scl, sclera. sp, spectacle. spi, spinal cord. te, tectum. tel, telencephalon. Reptile brain redrawn from Senn, D. G. (1979) in Gans, C. *et al.*, *Biology of the Reptilia*, Vol. 9, Academic Press, pp. 173–244. Lizard and snake eye redrawn from Bellairs, A. (1969) and amphisbaenian eye redrawn from Underwood, G. (1970) in Gans, C. and Parsons, T. S., *Biology of the Reptilia*, Vol. 2, Academic Press. pp. 1–97.

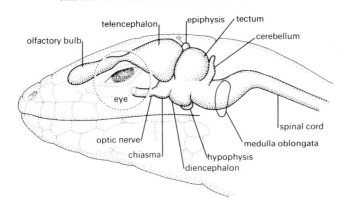

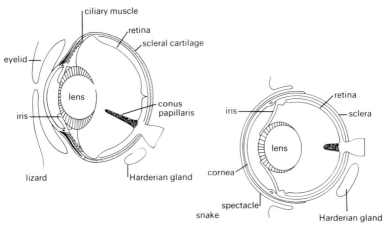

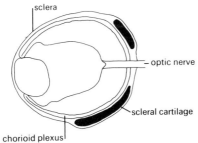

(Goldby and Gamble, 1957). The hemisphere is differentiated into dorsal pallial and ventral basal parts, and in adult reptiles the base of the hemisphere is connected to the hypothalamus by a continuous cell lamina. An interrelated set of structures, the parietal eye-pineal complex, has developed in the roof of the diencephalon of reptiles. This complex is dominated by two organs: the pineal organ or gland and the parietal eye. In the mesencephalon it is the tectum which processes both visual and non-visual sensory information related to movement. There are prominent optic lobes indicating a keen sense of vision. The rhombencephalon, which comprises about one-third of the total length of the brain, contains motor neurones innervating head muscles, as well as sensory nuclei. The cerebellum, a cortical structure positioned dorsally, is a centre for stimuli concerning the coordination of muscular movement.

The reptilian autonomic nervous system is very similar to that of mammals and includes the efferent nerve outflows which control involuntary tissues. In most reptiles there is a double trunk of nerves running the full length of the animal, and a bilateral system of segmentally arranged sympathetic ganglia.

Of all the sense organs, the eye is the most important for many reptiles. In general, most reptiles have movable upper and lower eyelids and a nictitating membrane which is usually transparent and can be moved across the cornea. In snakes and most burrowing lizards, the eye is covered by a transparent spectacle (brille) which presents a smooth external surface protecting the eye from injury (Figure 2.11). Chamaeleons have no nictitating membrane and the upper and lower eyelids are fused, leaving only a small hole the size of the pupil, and exposing the cornea. The majority of geckos have a transparent spectacle instead of movable eyelids, and their pupils have a series of serrations which provide a line of pinhole openings when the pupil is closed. This arrangement permits exceptionally good vision in poor light conditions. Accommodation in reptiles, other than snakes, is achieved by contraction of the ciliary muscle that presses the ciliary body against the peripheral edge of the elliptical lens. In snakes, accommodation is brought about by contraction of the iris and with forward movement of the lens for near vision. A special feature of chelonian eyes is the accommodation brought about by contraction of ciliary muscles and also of contraction of the iris sphincter, an adaptation for vision in air and in water. Cones are concerned chiefly with diurnal and colour vision and also visual activity, whereas rods are primarily used for night vision and to distinguish different light intensities. Both cones and rods are contained in the retina of *Sphenodon*, crocodilians and turtles.

Amongst the Squamata, the nocturnal species tend to have a predominance of rods.

Generally there are two main conjunctival glands, a Harderian gland at the front of the eye, and a lachrymal gland, usually at the back of the eye. In marine turtles the posterior lachrymal gland plays an important role in osmotic regulation. In lizards and snakes the lachrymal duct opens into the duct of Jacobson's organ or adjacent to it. In snakes the products of the Harderian glands flow into the lachrymal duct and then to the region of Jacobson's organ.

Sphenodon and many lizards possess a parietal or "median" eye, covered by a transparent scale, beneath a hole in the parietal bone. Studies of the parietal eye in *Sphenodon* have shown that there is a pigment layer of retina, a pineal eye lens and a pineal nerve connecting the parietal eye to the brain. No muscles have been found associated with this structure. Below and posterior to the parietal eye is the epiphysis, or pineal body, connected to the roof of the diencephalon by a solid stalk. Cells of the epiphysis bear some resemblance to those of the parietal eye retina and there is some evidence to suggest that the epiphysis was once an eye (Bellairs, 1969).

Despite an immense amount of research, the function and physiological relations of the parietal eye-pineal complex as a whole or its component parts is still to be settled. In a detailed review, Quay (1979) concludes that where the parietal eye occurs within reptilian groups it is either seen (living species) or suspected (extinct forms) to have its primary function as a photoreceptor, although entrainment of circadian activity in some lizards has been demonstrated to occur in blinded lizards, with the pineal organ and parietal eye removed (Underwood and Menaker, 1970). Quay suggests that functional overlap and replacement have occurred in those aspects of lateral eye function which do not involve imagery of visual fields, but which relate more to characteristics of ambient illumination. This in turn suggests that the photoreceptive parietal eye has diminished in most reptile groups, possibly in parallel with the advent of specialized subdivision of the accessory or non-visual inputs and projections from the lateral eyes.

A further suggestion is that possession of a parietal eye might facilitate survival of lizards at high latitudes where reproductive synchronization and thermoregulation are critical for reptiles (Gundy et al., 1975). This suggestion is based on the observation that lizards without parietal eyes tend to be restricted to low latitudes, whereas lizards with parietal eyes are successful at both low and high latitudes.

All reptiles have an inner ear and all, apart from snakes, have a middle ear. The tympanic membrane is often visible on the head and in some lizards it is covered by a scaly skin. Crocodilians have a slit-like external auditory meatus bounded frontally above and below by auricular appendages (ear-flaps). These may have a function in preventing injury to the tympanic membrane. The middle ear has considerable variation in reptiles (Wever, 1979). In snakes the middle ear cavity or tympanic cavity is obliterated, and the Eustachian tube is missing. Snakes therefore have been thought incapable of perceiving airborne vibrations, but may be able to receive vibrations conducted from the jaws via the columella and fenestra to the inner ear. Results from research by Wever and Vernon (1960) do not support the generally accepted view that snakes are deaf to aerial sounds, but indicate instead a narrow limitation in range. For low tones between 100 Hz and 700 Hz the snakes were found to be moderately sensitive both by air and bone conduction—the inferiority of a snake's hearing lies in its limited range and not in its absolute sensitivity. In crocodilians and most lizards the middle ear is analogous to that found in higher vertebrates. The inner ear has a general organization which corresponds to the typical vertebrate pattern, with three semicircular canals containing endolymph, and the cochlear duct. Some crocodilians and geckos are sensitive to sounds in the middle frequency range, but all other species of reptiles are sensitive to sounds in relatively restricted ranges of frequency, with low-range sounds being most easily detected. A detailed account of auditory sensitivity in reptiles has been provided by Belekhova (1979).

The nose in reptiles has a paired external nostril, often provided with a valve, and leads into a short chamber which then opens into the olfactory chamber lined with sensory epithelium and olfactory cells. Although there has been a development of a secondary palate and a more complicated nasal region compared to amphibians, it seems that only a small part of the lining of the nose has an olfactory function. However, associated with the reptile nose is the paired organ of Jacobson or vomeronasal organ. This is a modified part of the nasal cavity: in the Chelonia it is a small diverticulum but in the Squamata it is an independent chamber separated from the nasal cavity. In lizards and snakes Jacobson's organs (Figure 2.12) are important accessory olfactory organs used to detect airborne odours. Tongue flicking is partly associated with this function although not wholly necessary for the delivery of particles to Jacobson's organ (Halpern and Kubie, 1980). Bellairs (1969) suggested that secretions of the Harderian gland, after passing down the lachrymal duct, may also play a

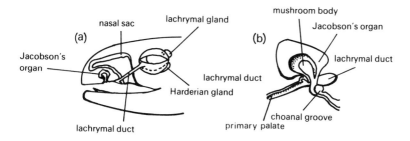

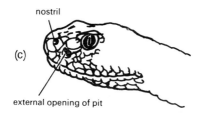

Figure 2.12 Diagrams showing Jacobson's organ of a lizard (*a*, *b*) and position of external opening of a sensory pit organ (*c*). (*a*) redrawn from Bellairs, A. (1969) *Life of Reptiles*; (*b*) redrawn from Bellairs, A. and Boyd, J. D. (1950) *Proc. Zool. Soc. London*, **120**, 269–310.

role in transmitting the odoriferous particles to the cavities of Jacobson's organ.

Paired heat-sensitive sensory pits (Figure 2.12) occur in snakes of the subfamily Crotalinae (pit vipers) between the eye and nostril, and rows of similar pits occur in the marginal scales of the jaws of some pythons and boas. The pit organs of crotaline snakes are highly sensitive to infra-red radiation. Those in *Python reticulatus* consist of a series of pits in the supralabial and infralabial scales. The morphology and the role of the pit organs in the feeding behaviour of *P. reticulatus* have been studied in depth by Bullock and Cowles (1952) and Buning *et al.* (1978).

CHAPTER THREE

PATTERNS OF DISTRIBUTION
AND ABUNDANCE

3.1 Introduction

The geographical distribution pattern of reptiles is particularly interesting from the point of view both of existing patterns and the factors which in the past have determined these patterns. Research on fossil material has provided good accounts of distribution during the Carboniferous, through the Mesozoic to the present. Continental drift probably had a major influence on the distribution and dispersion of reptiles, particularly from the Triassic to the end of the Cretaceous. After this, competition with other groups of animals and also climatic factors were probably of considerable importance; in more recent times, man has had a marked effect on the patterns of reptile distribution.

3.2 Past and present patterns of distribution

Chelonia

Continental drift and changes in climate may have had an important effect on the distribution of the Chelonia. Fossils of this group date back as far as the Late Triassic, but during the Jurassic period they radiated in a geographical and evolutionary sense. Two important suborders (Cryptodira and Pleurodira) evolved later along separate lines. During the Cretaceous and the early Tertiary the Pleurodira were present in North America and in Eurasia, but now they are restricted to southern continents. The suborder Pleurodira is essentially tropical and Webb *et al.* (1978) have suggested that the Pleurodira (but not the Cryptodira) were unable to survive the climatic changes that followed the movement of the land masses out of the tropical regions to the north temperate zones.

Fossils of the Cryptodira have been located in Upper Jurassic deposits, and were a dominant group in the northern hemisphere during the Upper Cretaceous. The suborder Cryptodira is represented in all zoogeographical regions but five families have a restricted distribution (Table 3.1).

Rhynchocephalia

The order Rhynchocephalia is thought by most to include five families, four of which are extinct. The one surviving species of the family Sphenodontidae, *Sphenodon punctatus* (the tuatara) is restricted in its distribution to a few islands off the New Zealand coast. This family has several extinct genera which were once widely distributed (except in North America) and fossils are known from deposits dating back to the Upper Triassic and the Upper Cretaceous. Other families such as Rhynchosauridae were also widely distributed and fossils have been found in many regions. *Sphenodon* of New Zealand is a classic example of a relict distribution, a sole survivor of an ancient group on some very old islands. The present reptile fauna of New Zealand consists of *Sphenodon* and both endemic and shared representatives of geckos and skinks (27 lizard species in total). The geckos are represented by three endemic genera with a total of ten species, the skinks by two genera both of which occur throughout the Australian and Oriental zoogeographical regions. It is possible that no large reptiles reached New Zealand and we could therefore speculate that elsewhere the slow-moving *Sphenodon* faced competition from the rich diversity of larger reptiles and also by the mammals. If the larger reptiles did reach New Zealand then there is no doubt that a deterioration in climate would not have favoured them, whereas *Sphenodon*, with a low voluntary temperature (Chapter 5), would have been at an advantage in a cool temperate climate. In more recent times *Sphenodon* has had a relatively widespread distribution in New Zealand, but anthropogenic factors and the introduction of terrestrial mammals have resulted in the now insular and restricted distribution of this species.

Squamata: Lacertilia

Like the Rhynchocephalia, the Squamata arose from Eosuchian stock during the Later Permian and Triassic geological periods. The suborder Lacertilia probably reached their peak of adaptive radiation in more recent times. The present distribution of living families is shown in Table 3.1 and a more detailed description of the larger families follows below.

Table 3.1   Zoogeographical distribution of reptilian families

	Palearctic	Ethiopian	Oriental	Australian	Neoarctic	Neotropical	Madagascar*	New Zealand*
Order Chelonia								
Suborder Pleurodira								
Family Pelomedusidae		●				○	●	
„ Chelidae				●		●		
Suborder Cryptodira								
Family Emydidae	○	●	●		○	●	●	
„ Testudinidae	○	●	●		○	●	●	
„ Platysternidae			○					
„ Chelydridae					○	•		
„ Kinosternidae					○	○		
„ Dermatemydidae						•		
„ Cheloniidae	•	○	●	○	•	○	○	
„ Dermochelyidae			○		•	○		
„ Carettochelyidae			•					
„ Trionychidae	○	●	●		○	○		
Order Rhynchocephalia								
Family Sphenodontidae								●
Order Squamata								
Suborder Lacertilia								
Family Gekkonidae	○	●	●	●	•	●	●	●
„ Pygopodidae				●				
„ Xantusiidae					•	•		
„ Dibamidae			○					
„ Anelytropsidae						•		
„ Iguanidae				•	○	●	●	
„ Agamidae	○	●	●	●				
„ Chamaeleontidae	○	●	○				●	
„ Scincidae	○	●	●	●	○	●	●	●
„ Lacertidae	●	●	●					
„ Teiidae					○	●		
„ Feylinidae		●						
„ Cordylidae		●					●	
„ Anguidae	○		○		○	●		
„ Anniellidae					•			
„ Xenosauridae			•			•		
„ Varanidae	○	●	●	●				
„ Helodermatidae					•			
„ Lanthanotidae			•					
Suborder Amphisbaenia								
Family Bipedidae					•			
„ Amphisbaenidae	○	●			•	●		
„ Trogonophidae	○	○						

Table 3.1—*continued*

	Palearctic	Ethiopian	Oriental	Australian	Neoarctic	Neotropical	Madagascar*	New Zealand*
Suborder Ophidia								
Family Anomalepidae						●		
„ Typhlopidae	○	●	●	●	•	●	●	●
„ Leptotyphlopidae		●	•			•	●	
„ Aniliidae			○			○		
„ Uropeltidae			○					
„ Boidae	○	●	●	●		○	●	●
„ Xenopeltidae			●					
„ Acrochordidae			●	○				
„ Colubridae	●	●	●	●		●	●	●
„ Elapidae	•	●	●	●		•	●	
„ Viperidae	●	●	●			●	●	
Order Crocodilia								
Family Crocodylidae		●	●	○		•	●	●
„ Gavialidae			○					

● Representatives in most of the region.
○ Representatives in about half the region.
• Representatives in a small part of the region.

* Madagascar and New Zealand are treated separately because of their long isolation.

The same procedure follows for the snakes (i.e. distribution of the smaller families is not discussed in the text).

Fossils of the family Gekkonidae are known from the Eocene of Europe and living representatives are found throughout the zoogeographical regions and on the old islands of Madagascar and New Zealand (Table 3.1). The New Zealand geckos are the only members of this large and diverse family that give birth to live young. This group in particular has been aided in its dispersal by man's activities—for instance, geckos are frequently found in ship's cargo.

The Iguanidae is a large, well-known family of lizards well represented in the Neotropical and Neoarctic region and also in Madagascar and the Fiji Islands. Some fossil material has been recorded and it would seem that despite the geographical distribution of living forms, the Iguanids did occur at one time on the Old World continents.

The Agamidae are ecologically and morphologically similar to the Iguanidae, but in contrast they are represented in much of the Palearctic

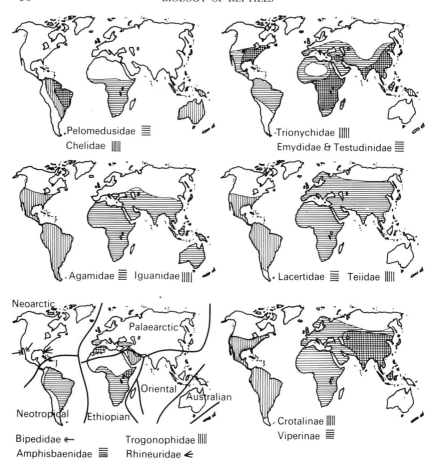

Figure 3.1 Distribution of some reptile groups and the zoogeographical regions.

and throughout the Ethiopian, Oriental and Australian zoogeographical regions (Figure 3.1, Table 3.1). Adaptive radiation of the two groups almost certainly occurred after the Americas drifted westward. Fossil agamids have been found in the Eocene deposits of Europe.

Fossils of the family Chamaeleontidae are known from the Pleistocene deposits of south-western Asia and the Upper Cretaceous deposits of eastern Asia. The distribution of the living forms is not extensive—they occur in the Ethiopian, Oriental, south-western areas of the Palearctic regions and on the island of Madagascar.

In contrast to the Chamaeleontidae, the Scincidae is a cosmopolitan family with a widespread distribution throughout the zoogeographical regions (Table 3.1). With a total of about 800 species this family has been remarkably successful. Representatives of this large family have been recovered from Eocene deposits of Europe and from Cretaceous deposits of the Neoarctic.

The ecology and geographical distribution of the families Teiidae (whiptail lizards) and Lacertidae compare well with the two families Iguanidae and Agamidae. Found in the Neotropical and Neoarctic, the Teiidae is a large group of lizards and fossil examples are known from Cretaceous deposits of the same regions. Lacertids, which are remarkably similar ecologically and morphologically to the Teiidae, are found today in the Palearctic, Ethiopian and Oriental zoogeographical regions. It is interesting to note that fossils of this group are known from the Upper Jurassic and Miocene deposits of Europe.

The family Cordylidae are scincomorph lizards represented by about 10 living genera and are restricted to the Ethiopian region and Madagascar. The genus *Gerrhosaurus* is a well-known representative from southern Africa, and fossils of this species have been recorded from Miocene deposits in the same region. Some extinct genera are known from the Upper Jurassic and Eocene deposits in Europe.

The Anguidae are known from Cretaceous deposits of North America and the Middle Eocene of Europe. Living forms (about ten genera) are found mostly in the Neotropical region: one (*Anguis*) is found only in Europe and western Asia, and *Ophisaurus* is found in Asia, North America and south-eastern Europe. Whereas some have well developed limbs (Alligator lizards, *Gerrhonotus*) both *Anguis* and *Ophisaurus* are limbless.

The family Varanidae is known from fossils found in Upper Tertiary deposits in Europe, Southern Asia, Australia, Africa and the East Indies. Usually a single genus (*Varanus*) is included in this family and these lizards are ecologically similar to the mammalian carnivores. They are widely distributed in the Ethiopian, Oriental, Australian regions and also in southern parts of the Palearctic. The famous *Varanus komodensis* or "Komodo dragon" of Indonesia reaches a length of about 3 m and is thus the largest living lizard.

Squamata: Amphisbaenia

Four families of living representatives of the suborder Amphisbaenia are currently recognized (Figure 3.1): the Bipedidae occur in Mexico; the

Amphisbaenidae have a widespread distribution in the Neotropical and southern parts of the Ethiopian regions, and also occur in the warm temperate regions of Europe; the Trogonophidae are found only in north-western Africa, the horn of Africa and in areas around the Persian Gulf; and the Rhineuridae are restricted to some localities in Florida. Gans (1979) has suggested that although the earliest known Amphisbaenia date back to the Eocene, the three squamate suborders separated well before the Cretaceous.

Squamata: Ophidia

The Leptotyphlopidae (slender blind snakes) are today found in both the Neotropical and the Ethiopian regions (except the Sahara). The distribution of this and other families is somewhat perplexing because, from what little fossil material is available, it seems that snakes arose towards the end of the Mesozoic. Yet, by the end of the Cretaceous, the south Atlantic was a major ocean. During the Tertiary it may have been possible for some families of snakes to somehow cross the oceans. It would also seem likely that some families arose in the Old World, then spread northwards and westwards to the Nearctic where fossils of primitive snakes have been found.

One of the most widely distributed families is the Boidae (Table 3.1). Both living representatives and fossil representatives are known from most tropical and subtropical regions of the world. The family includes small and medium-sized snakes as well as the largest snakes. One particularly interesting subfamily is the Bolyeriinae, restricted to Round Island, near Mauritius. This group has no vestige of a hind limb and the upper jaw has a somewhat unusual arrangement in that a supplementary linkage allows the jaw to divide into a front and rear segment. The Round Island boas are also notable in that special conservation measures have been taken to ensure their survival (Chapter 8).

The family Colubridae includes most of the living snakes. Fossils are known from Miocene deposits in North America, Europe and eastern Asia. It is a very successful family, there is notable ecological diversity and several subfamilies are recognized.

The Elapidae include a number of subfamilies, some of which have adaptations for a marine existence. Fossils are known from the Pliocene of North America and the Pleistocene of Europe. The subfamily Elapinae are predominant in the Australian region but are also found in other areas especially the tropical and subtropical regions. The Hydrophiinae or sea snakes have affinities with the elapids of Australia (Dunson, 1975; Mao and Chen, 1980). They are distributed throughout tropical and subtropical areas of the Pacific and Indian Ocean.

The Viperidae is another widely distributed family (although not Australian) with particularly interesting northern distribution limits—the snake *Vipera berus* is found as far north as 65–67°N in Russia. Fossils of the genus *Vipera* are known from Miocene deposits of Europe. The Crotalines or pit vipers are found predominantly in the New World, but some are also known from the Oriental region and eastern Palaearctic.

Crocodilia

The present distribution of the crocodiles and that of the alligators and caimans does not overlap except in central America. The former (crocodiles) are found in Ethiopia, Oriental and some parts of the Australian region while the latter (alligators and caimans) are found in the Neotropical and in southern China. The caimans are Neotropical alligators, and the sole member of the Gavialidae (*Gavialis gangeticus*), the gavial or "gharial", is found only in India and Burma. The Crocodilia have ancestral origins going back to the Triassic and are the only archosaurians to survive to the present time. The fossils of this group have been extensively studied and are known from deposits from the Triassic through to the Cretaceous in several regions. It is probable that the primitive stock lived in the Neotropical region, and that expansion of the Eosuchia occurred during the late Cretaceous and the early part of the Tertiary. Sill (1968) concluded that the present distribution is essentially a relic of that which existed during the early Tertiary.

3.3 Spatial patterns

The total number of species in an area is called the *species richness*, whereas *species diversity* is measured by weighting the contributions of species according to their relative abundance. It is perhaps to be expected that reptile species richness will vary from region to region, although the underlying ecological factors are less obvious. The tropical regions and the desert regions have by far the highest levels of reptile species richness but this diminishes in the temperate climatic regions. The number of reptile species found on different islands is a further and interesting topic and this aspect has contributed much to the studies of island ecology and island biogeography.

Latitudinal gradients

Although the phenomenon of latitudinal gradients in animal and plant species richness has long been recognized, the patterns are far from perfect. Irregularities arise from factors such as spatial heterogeneity, niche and competition, predation, productivity, time since occupation and rates of extinction and colonization. Although there is no distinct, generally distributed zonal pattern of reptile fauna in the northern regions, Darlington (1957) concluded that reptiles do have an overall zonal pattern of distribution. There are far more reptile species in the tropical regions than in the temperate regions and a pattern of decreasing species richness has been recorded for some lizard and some snake species (Dobzhansky, 1950).

Zonal patterns of reptile species richness in the western areas of the Palearctic zoogeographical region provide a good example (Figure 3.2). An explanation for this pattern of increasing number of species from north

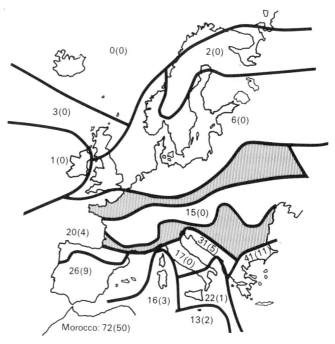

Figure 3.2   Numbers of reptile species (excluding marine tortoises and introduced species) in various regions of Britain and Europe. The first figure is the total number of species and the second figure is the total number not found elsewhere in Europe. Shaded areas are regions where there is a complex transition in number of reptile species. Prepared by N. D. Smith.

to south might be based on the period of time since the last glaciation. The reptile fauna in this region (encompassed by the Arctic Circle, British Isles, the Mediterranean and Russia) is a relatively recent complex. From about 12 000 to 10 000 years BP (before present) reptiles would have been able to move northwards following the retreat of the last of the four recent major glacial periods. Britain separated from continental Europe about 7500 years ago. This has provided a classic example of recent continental island faunal patterns. Two aspects are apparent: firstly, in the short time of about 10 000 years there has been an invasion of reptile species northwards, but insufficient time has elapsed for a large number of species to colonize the northern regions; secondly, reptiles are ectothermic and so are limited by low temperatures.

A time theory has indeed been proposed, by both zoogeographers and paleontologists, as an explanation for latitudinal gradients in species richness. Pianka (1966) suggested that ecological and evolutionary processes should however be distinguished. That is, ecological processes would apply where a species has not had time to disperse into a relatively newly available area. Evolutionary processes apply to longer time spans where a newly available habitat is not yet utilized, but will, through speciation and evolution eventually be occupied. The former could well apply to the reptiles of north-western Europe and the latter might be applicable to the lizard fauna of Australian deserts where the last glaciation occurred around 60 000 years or more BP.

A further explanation involves spatial heterogeneity. Proponents of this theory claim that the more heterogeneous and complex the physical environment, the more complex the animal and plant species communities, and therefore the higher the species richness. There is evidence to show that bird species richness in some areas is related to the structural diversity of the plant communities (McArthur, 1972). As yet there has been little attempt to relate latitudinal species richness gradients of reptiles to the spatial heterogeneity of the habitats in northern zoogeographical regions. However, Pianka (1967), who has examined many species of desert lizards in western North America, concluded that increased spatial heterogeneity of the vegetation was a major factor allowing coexistence of more species in the south.

Habitats and species richness

My own observations confirm that the lizard fauna in parts of the Australian deserts and neighbouring regions is very rich. This example

Figure 3.3   A community of *Triodea* in the Little Desert of South Australia.

prompts questions as to why these areas support such a high species richness, how the species coexist, and whether there is competitive exclusion? These questions can be answered, at least in part, from studies of the plant life forms in habitats with high reptile species richness and by comparisons with other regions. For example, one plant unique to Australia is *Triodea*, popularly known as spinifex (Figure 3.3), a perennial grass which grows as dense clumps in desert regions. In one spinifex community in the Great Victorian desert, Pianka (1969, 1977) found as many as 16 species of lizards. Some very interesting comparisons between the large number of lizard species in Australian deserts and the comparatively low numbers in North America have been noted by Pianka. Firstly, Australian desert snake and mammal fauna is comparatively impoverished; the lizards could be thought to take the role of other taxa (for example, the large monitor lizard, *Varanus gouldii*, could be an ecological analogue of the kit fox, *Vulpes macrotis*, of western North America). Further, it was found that when the number of snake-like lizard species (pygopodids) was added to the number of snake species, Australian and North American "snake" species densities were comparable. Partitioning of environmental resources temporally as well as spatially could be one important factor in view of the observation that there are many nocturnal Australian lizard species compared with the few found in North America (Chapter 6). As Pianka observed, as many as 11 species may occur sympatrically in the Australian desert, and the stenotypic habits of genera such as *Ctenotus* may also contribute to the high species richness. The coexistence of so many species is astonishing and may perhaps be partly explained by differences in voluntary temperatures (Chapter 5). Perhaps the most important factor, however, is that the desert environments of Australia are spatially and structurally more heterogeneous than those of North America. The unique structure of *Triodea* contributes much to the heterogeneity and this, coupled with a long history and fairly uniform climate, has provided conditions for a high level of lizard species richness.

3.4   Distribution and species richness on islands

What factors determine the number and composition of species on an island and what factors determine the equilibrium number of species? In very simple terms, the equilibrium number of species tends to increase if the source of colonization is close, is rich in number of species, or is a large area or zoogeographical region; if the island is large, has a stable environment and has a high level of spatial heterogeneity. Examples taken from studies of reptiles (and amphibians) on islands very well exemplify some basic principles of island biogeography.

History and colonization

The faunal composition of recent continental islands is typically an impoverished version of the nearby zoogeographical region and is determined in part by historical factors, climate, corridors and barriers. For example the present distribution of reptiles in the British Isles (Figure 3.4) could be the result of a gradual colonization beginning about 15 000 years BP followed by the extinction and retreat of some species. A possible sequence of events may have been as follows. About 15 000 years BP the climate in northern Europe was beginning to become warmer and with a land corridor extending across the Channel, some reptiles (e.g. *Lacerta vivipara*) colonized the area which was later to become the British Isles. From about 11 000 years BP and during the next few thousand years, some species reached Ireland and Scotland, while others (*Anguis fragilis*, *Vipera berus*) would have colonized at least the southern regions of the British

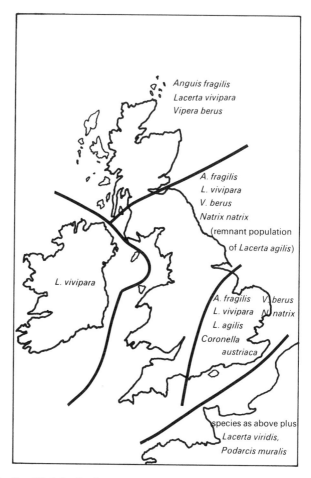

Figure 3.4 Simplified distribution map of reptiles in Britain, showing a latitudinal gradient in species richness.

Isles. The arrival and success of these reptiles from then onwards was very much linked to changes in climate and in the species composition of the vegetation. From about 10 000 to 7000 years BP there were flourishing birch (*Betula*) forests followed by hazel (*Corylus*) and conifers in many areas of Britain: the climate had entered a warm phase. This warm climate would have favoured the reptiles and during very hot periods they would be able to retreat to the woodlands. Between 8000 and 7000 years BP the sea level rose to an extent which isolated Britain from the continent, creating the English Channel: this provided a barrier which prevented the arrival of any further reptile species. By that time there may have been as many as eight reptile species (including *Natrix natrix*, *Coronella austriaca*, *Podarcis muralis*, and *Lacerta viridis*) in the British Isles. Today the two species *Podarcis muralis* and *Lacerta viridis* are found only on the Channel Islands and in continental Europe. From about 5000 years BP onwards, man was to have an important impact on the woodlands by way of clearing and this, together with a climatic deterioration between 3000 and 2000 years BP would have caused some species to become extinct in Britain or to survive only in southern and warmer areas.

Beebee (1978) suggested a sequence of events similar to that already described with the object of explaining the distribution of Britain's rare reptiles (*Lacerta agilis* and *Coronella austriaca*). An alternative hypothesis and one based on detailed botanical evidence has been proposed by Yalden (1980). He suggested that between 10 600 and 10 000 years BP the climate was far too cold for reptiles to inhabit Britain. Between 10 000 and 9000 years BP the reptiles would have reacted quickly to the arrival of warm climate and would have colonized areas as far north as north-west England. It seems that there was a short period around 9500 years BP when the climate had improved rapidly, although forest cover had not yet spread to Britain. The subsequent development of forest cover would have restricted some reptile species to small refuges of open habitat, perhaps dune systems or around early human settlements. The distribution and abundance of Britain's reptiles have more recently been harmfully affected by afforestation, agriculture, urbanization and the construction of motorways.

Patterns of colonization on island archipelagos make an interesting comparison with that described above. For example, the ecology and zoogeography of the iguanid *Anolis* lizards in the West Indies have received much attention in recent years, and Williams (1969) has published a detailed and useful summary, with particular reference to small islands. The West Indies is ecologically rich and varied and embraces five subregions: Greater Antilles, Bahamas, Western Caribbean, Southern Caribbean, Lesser Antilles. There are relatively few islands on the continental shelf (all are small) and those not now on the shelf had no mainland connection. Etheridge (1960) used osteological characters as a basis for describing relationships of *Anolis* lizards in the Caribbean. The major osteological character is the presence (β) or absence (α) of a transverse process on distal caudal vertebrae. Subsequently Gorman and his colleagues contributed much information to an understanding of the relationships and zoogeography of Caribbean *Anolis* lizards (see for example Gorman and Atkins, 1969; Gorman and Dessauer, 1965). Origins and dispersal of the anoles can only be speculated on but it is probable that one section (β) are Mexican–Central American endemics which reached the western Antilles and successfully invaded the South American mainland after the close of the Panama gap in the late Pliocene. The other section (α) are South American endemics which have invaded the Antilles and eventually Cuba and the United States.

The most successful of the colonizers is *Anolis carolinensis* (common green anole). This species group, once it had originated in Cuba as a relatively primitive derivative of an early arboreal α section, differentiated, dispersed and colonized many islands. Only *Anolis sagrei* (β section), also of Cuban origin, has been equally successful and has similarly spread outward from the islands toward the mainland. The *carolinensis* complex and *A. sagrei* are sympatric throughout Cuba where the latter has a clear niche difference, being found on lower trunks and on the ground. No other anoles are comparable to *A. carolinensis* and *A. sagrei* as colonizers; all the others are established on only one or a few islands.

The general conclusions reached by Williams have been based on the colonization by *Anolis* lizards of small and distant islands (never connected to dry land and always requiring dispersal over water). A small fraction of existing species are effective colonizers—for example, in the Greater Antilles (Cuba, Hispaniola, Puerto Rico, Jamaica, St Croix) about six of at least 56 species have colonized the recently available small islands. Of importance, these are eurytopic species inhabiting ecotones and have the ability to colonize temporarily open habitats. The factors of distance, currents and vagility seem to have been important in preventing colonization by other mainland species. The highly vagile species include *A. carolinensis* and *A. sagrei*, which are inhabitants of open forest and savannah and not deep shade, rain forest or montane areas. This suggests that they would be relatively resistant to desiccation and would therefore be able to tolerate the conditions of rafting between islands. Coexistence of colonists is possible if the colonizing species have been preadapted in sympatry on ecologically more complex source islands and if, arriving nearly synchronously, they maintain essentially the same ecological relationships they had on the source islands. Coexistence may also be involved *in situ* in the special circumstances of complex geography including complex island banks—circumstances which remind us of the sympatric species of lizards inhabiting the structurally complex areas of Australian deserts.

Area

The area of an island is one aspect of insular ecology which seems to have a profound effect on the equilibrium number of species. Numerous studies on reptiles and amphibians have provided material for species area curves (Figure 3.5). In this example the island of Trinidad has a high species richness for its area. This could partly be explained by the richness of plant communities on the island and also by the complex topographical relief affording a good spatial heterogeneity, which in turn would provide a large number of habitats suitable for reptiles and amphibians. In general, large islands may contain more species (of a particular taxon) than small islands and this relationship can be expressed by the simple equation

$$S = CA^k$$

where S is the number of species, C is a constant giving the number of species when A has a value of one, A is the area of the island and k is the slope of the regression line. Values of k for real islands fall within the range 0.24–0.34.

The graph in Figure 3.5 suggests however that the species–area curve should not be considered independent of habitat diversity. Area, habitat diversity and other characteristics of an island all play a role in determining the number of species on an island. Many characteristics of the species are also important and so also are rates of extinction and immigration. MacArthur and Wilson (1967) developed a simple model to explain the variation in the number of species on islands. This model

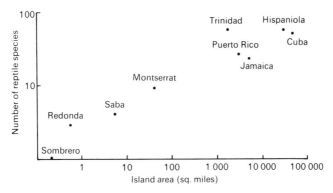

Figure 3.5 Log-log plot of reptile species richness against island area. Data from Darlington, P. J. (1957) *Zoogeography*, John Wiley & Son.

represents the number of species on an island as a dynamic equilibrium resulting from the continuing process of immigration and extinction. Island size has little effect on immigration rate, but decreasing island size affects the rate of extinction. A further factor is introduced by this model; the rate of turnover or species replacement depends on characteristics of the island. MacArthur and Wilson's model has been an incentive for a wide range of ecological research including the application of island biogeographical theory to biological conservation (Wilcox, 1980), and some reptile communities have benefited in terms of conservation either directly or indirectly from this type of research.

CHAPTER FOUR

REPRODUCTION AND DEVELOPMENT

4.1   Sexual dimorphism and sexual maturity

It is generally the case that in most species of reptiles, the sexes are of different sizes. Amongst the Chelonia, the males of many aquatic species are smaller than females whereas males of terrestrial species typically grow larger than females. Berry and Shine (1980) have drawn attention to correlations between size dimorphism and sexual behaviour in the Chelonia in terms of sexual selection theory. In those species where the male is larger than the female, the male size is thought to have evolved as an adaptation to increase success in male combats. (Male combat and forcible insemination are rare in aquatic species but instead there are elaborate precoital displays.) The small males of aquatic species have evolved, on the other hand, to increase the male's efficiency in locating the larger female.

One of the characteristics of the unique reptile *Sphenodon* is that the sexes are similar; the male lacks copulatory organs, and there are few external indications of sexual dimorphism. The Maori name "tuatara" refers to the folds of skin which in the male form a conspicuous dorsal crest; in the female, this crest is rudimentary. Normally flaccid, this crest in the male can be stiffened and erected when the animal has been disturbed.

Amongst the Lacertilia, the male is often the larger sex but there are many exceptions. There is, in some lizard species, a difference between sexes in head width of the adults, the males having a slightly larger head. It seems that adult males of some species select larger prey than taken by females, as in for example, adult males of *Anolis conspersus*, which have a head size 1.3 to 1.5 times that of females (see Chapter 6).

Perhaps most obvious in some species is the pre-nuptial integument colour, or a marked difference in colour of male and female lizards. Prominent colours on the flanks (an emerald green in *Lacerta agilis*) or patches of bright colours on the head (as in *Agama agama*) may be important in conflict and in courtship behaviour.

Female snakes are often the larger sex but their tail is generally shorter than that of the male and lacks a penial swelling. In many species a difference in the number of sub-caudal scales can be a good indication of the sex: males of some species tend to have a greater number of sub-caudal scales than do the females. There are few other examples of sexual dimorphism in snakes and the exceptions are therefore particularly interesting. The tree-climbing colubrid *Langaha nasuta* of Madagascar is unusual in that nasal processes in males have a simple round peg-shaped structure whereas in females the nasal process is rather like a fleshy torn leaf. *Vipera berus* shows an interesting sexual dimorphism in colour. Females tend to be red, reddish brown or golden with darker red or brown patterns and males are generally yellow, pale grey or light olive with black markings.

As the rate of growth of reptiles is highly variable, sexual maturity is linked more closely to stage of development or size rather than to age in years. In specialized studies it is therefore useful to record size and age (if possible) when determining sexual maturity. As a general guide it seems that sexual maturity in the Chelonia is reached after about three years. However, in some species, for example desert tortoises (e.g. *Gopherus agassize*) sexual maturity is not reached until about the age of 15 years. *Sphenodon* has a particularly low growth rate and sexual maturity is not reached until about 20 years of age. Amongst the suborder Lacertilia, sexual maturity is often reached after about one or two years, despite considerable variation between species: in the side-blotched lizard *Uta stansburiana*, females can be sexually mature at four months, but in the case of the slow-worm or legless lizard (*Anguis fragilis*) it may be three or four years. There is also considerable variation amongst the Ophidia, but two to three years seems to be the general rule, and they generally take longer to become sexually mature than lizards. Amongst the crocodiles, sexual maturity is generally not reached until after about 10 to 15 years; in alligators, it is about 6 to 10 years.

4.2 Reproductive cycles

In most reptiles there is a regular reproductive cycle which includes a seasonal pattern of gonadal activity. Exceptions include the lizards

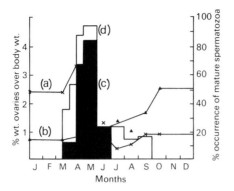

Figure 4.1 Reproductive cycle in the snake *Vipera berus*. Graphs (*a*) and (*b*) show seasonal changes in weight of ovaries for (*a*) breeding adult females and (*b*) non-breeding females which will breed the following year. Histograms are for breeding periods of males shown by (*c*) abundant mature spermatozoa and (*d*) small quantities of spermatozoa in the vasa deferentia of adult males. Redrawn from Prestt, I. (1971) *J. Zool., Lond.*, **164**, 373–418.

Cyrtodactylus and *Draco* found in the rain forests of Borneo. These lizards have no seasonal patterns of egg production and males are capable of sperm production throughout the year (Inger and Greenberg, 1966). Although seasonal patterns of reproductive activity are known to occur in many reptiles, it is important that the young are born at the optimum time for their survival. In reptiles, as in many other vertebrates, environmental factors control the reproductive cycle and it has been possible to determine which factors synchronize the reproductive cycle to seasonal events. In the following few examples we see that although the reproductive cycle of many reptiles follows a similar plan, there are many interesting adaptive modifications (Fitch, 1970).

The pattern of gonadal activity of the snake *Vipera berus* has been studied in detail (Prestt, 1971) and the seasonal change in the ovaries can be determined by expressing the weight of the ovaries as a percentage of body weight (Figure 4.1). Females of this species in continental Europe breed every year, but for this and other species inhabiting more northerly regions, there is a biennial cycle (exceptionally a three-year cycle). The time between emergence and the commencement of winter dormancy is too short at high latitudes for these females to undergo a regular annual reproductive cycle. In the period between birth and overwintering, females are incapable of locating sufficient food to completely replenish energy reserves used for reproduction. The breeding cycle of the male *V. berus* (based on the presence or absence of mature spermatozoa in the vasa deferentia of adult males) reaches a peak in April–May (Figure 4.1). In contrast, the production of spermatozoa by adult males of *Coronella austriaca* (geographical distribution overlaps with *V. berus*) remains at a constant level throughout the summer and it appears that mating can occur at any time during their activity period. Kellerway and Brain (1978) have described seasonal variations in testicular histology of the adult male *V. berus* and they suggest that while changing temperature levels may break dormancy by activating the thyroid, testicular activity is more closely related to changing photoperiod in the spring and the late autumn.

The reproductive cycle of the anolis lizard *Anolis carolinensis* from the south-eastern United States is prolonged, as is evident from the egg-laying

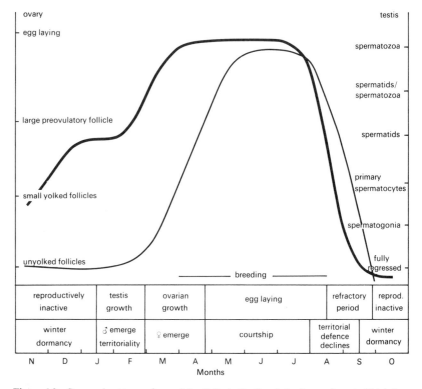

Figure 4.2 Seasonal patterns of gonadal activity in the lizard *Anolis carolinensis*. Thick line, sequence of events for males and thin line for females. Redrawn from Crews, D. (1975) *Science*, **189**, 1059–1065.

period which extends from April to August. In adult females a single ovarian follicle develops into an egg every ten to fourteen days (Figure 4.2). Licht's (1971) observations show that males are potentially continuous breeders, but the synchrony of the annual testis cycle with changing seasons depends on a shift from a physiological phase where temperature is the main factor, to a phase when photoperiod is dominant. Female *A. carolinensis* maintained under constant environmental conditions undergo three to four complete ovarian cycles per year suggesting that seasonal ovarian growth and regression is partly under endogenous control. However, Crews (1975) has discovered that the males' ability to extend the dewlap (a brightly coloured gular fan) is important in male facilitation of ovarian recrudescence and in mate selection.

Research on the lizard *Uta stansburiana* has shown that photoperiod does not affect timing of the female reproductive cycle. Tinkle and Irwin (1965) found that in laboratory studies, they could initiate a reproductive cycle in *U. stansburiana* with prolonged periods of temperature above 27°C regardless of the photoperiod.

There is no doubt that temporal aspects of reptilian reproductive cycles are controlled primarily by changing photoperiod with some modifications resulting from changing temperature cycles. Other physical factors such as precipitation have little effect on reproductive cycles; seasonal changes in the abundance of food may however affect timing and onset of breeding. For example the breeding season of the agamid *Agama agama* in Ghana has two peaks, each preceded by a rainy season (Chapman and Chapman, 1964). Following periods of rain there is a great increase in the abundance of invertebrates and the breeding of this lizard therefore coincides with a seasonal abundance of food.

4.3 Natality

Most lizard species in temperate climatic regions have a short annual breeding cycle resulting in one clutch each year. In some tropical and subtropical species there may be more than one clutch each year: for example, some species of *Cnemidophorus* produce two or sometimes three clutches. The common anole of the south-eastern United States (*Anolis carolinensis*) in some localities has a breeding season extending from mid-spring to the end of summer. Eggs are laid singly and at intervals of about two weeks. In other *Anolis* species, up to eight clutches can be produced each season. In the majority of snakes and lizards there is one clutch each year:

unfortunately information on species laying more than one clutch is limited. Based on Porter's (1972) extensive literature review, the mean minimum number of young or eggs produced in each clutch by lizards is 4.8 and the mean maximum is 11.4. Snakes seem to be more prolific than lizards: their mean minimum is 6.2 and the mean maximum is 23.8.

The freshwater turtles and land tortoises produce clutches of less than 20 eggs, but some can lay more than one clutch each year. In contrast, the marine turtles produce large clutches. Green turtles (*Chelonia mydas*), for example, lay several times in a year and there may be as many as 100–200 eggs per clutch. The incidence of predation of marine turtle eggs and hatchlings is obviously important and is related to the high number of eggs laid by marine turtles. American alligators deposit between 15 and 88 eggs per clutch (average 35) and this is not an unusual number for a member of the Crocodilia. Although the Nile crocodile (*Crocodylus niloticus*) has a fairly definite breeding season it comes at different times in different regions; on average, 60 eggs per clutch are produced.

4.4   Mode of reproduction

Oviparity

The reptile egg, with an outer protective parchment or calcareous shell and three internal membranes, was an important adaptation during the transition from an aquatic to a terrestrial environment. The amphibian egg lacks an outer protective shell and is anamniotic, whereas reptiles and birds have an amniotic egg. Most modern reptiles are oviparous: the Rhynchocephalia, Crocodilia, Chelonia and many of the Squamata lay eggs. However, squamate evolution resulted in many viviparous forms and a few in which different levels of placentation are known to occur. Despite some variation in size, shape and shell texture, eggs of different reptile species are remarkably similar.

Typically, the eggs of oviparous reptiles have a shell, a chorion which encloses the embryo and yolk, a sac-like allantois in which waste products are stored, and an amnion which envelops the embryo (Figure 4.4). The shell, composed of layers of alternating fibres, is secreted by specialized glands in the oviduct, and in oviparous reptiles the outer layers are impregnated with calcium salts. Albumen is secreted by the oviductal wall and serves as a water reserve, but there is an abundant supply only in the Chelonia and the Crocodilia. The formation and function of albumen in the reptile egg may in some instances be connected with mechanisms to resist desiccation. Badham's work (1971) on the agamid *Amphibolurus barbatus*, showed that albumen is absent from newly-laid eggs, but when they are incubated in moist sand, a clear viscous fluid develops surrounding the embryo and yolk. She concluded from subsequent investigations that the parchment-shelled eggs of this agamid take up water, and that this results in the formation of an albumen layer whose colloidal properties function to resist desiccation. The yolk is the main source of food for the embryo and is contained in the yolk sac entering the body of the embryo at the umbilicus. The yolk consists mainly of combined fat and protein (lipoproteins) but also contains calcium, phosphorus and other minerals which are utilized for skeletal ossification.

Despite the presence of three membranes and the outer shell, eggs can lose water after laying even if the atmospheric water vapour pressure is high. At the same time, however, water can be taken up by eggs when in direct contact with a moist substratum. The rate of water uptake is determined in part by the physical properties of the soil. Similarly the rate of embryonic development is determined partly by the thermal characteristics of the substratum. It seems therefore that the level of incubation success and the condition of the hatchlings is related to the water and thermal characteristics of the substratum.

From time to time there are reports of reptile eggs hatching not in late summer, but early the following spring, with the explanation that late summer weather conditions slowed development and that hatching was delayed until the return of suitable thermal conditions. Gibbons and Nelson (1978) found that overwintering of the eggs of five species of temperate zone turtles from the south-eastern United States is in fact typical of most species of aquatic turtles indigenous to that region. They concluded that hatchlings opting for immediate emergence from the eggs are more likely to encounter high risks in the environment and are therefore usually selected against. Delayed hatching and emergence from the nest allows the young to benefit from rapid growth and suffer less impact from predation and adverse environmental conditions.

All crocodilians are oviparous and females construct nests for their eggs. Species such as the American alligator (*Alligator mississippiensis*), the crocodile, *Crocodylus porosus*, and some caimans, construct large elaborate nests from mixtures of vegetation and mud. Chelonians are also oviparous and females deposit eggs in prepared nest sites. Active selection of nest sites is not uncommon and certain beaches are known to be regularly used by large numbers of marine turtles. Desiccation of embryos is prevented by some species by the habit of using bladder water to moisten the nest. Selection of nest sites by oviparous lizards is also a fairly common feature. Several species excavate in sand or soil for the construction of nest sites (e.g. the sand lizard, *Lacerta agilis*, and the Indian spiny-tailed lizard, *Uromastyx hardwickii*); some lay eggs beneath rock exfoliations or bark (e.g. the Australian lizard, *Pseudemoia spenceri*, and many gecko species); and others select sites under or in logs (e.g. water teiids such as *Neusticurus*). Some of the larger lizards deposit eggs in the shelter provided by termite nests (e.g. the Nile monitor *Varanus niloticus*, and large teiids such as the tegus *Tupinambis* of central and northern South America). Some of the oviparous snakes such as *Natrix natrix* will travel some distance before selecting suitable nest sites in warm and moist locations. A few snakes, such as the king cobra *Ophiophagus hannah*, actually construct nest sites from vegetation, but nest building among snakes seems to be rare. Female pythons have been known to remain with their eggs until they hatch. The Indian python *Python molurus* is able to raise her body temperature to levels slightly above that of the surroundings and so assist the incubation process.

Viviparity and egg retention

Whereas most reptiles are oviparous, some lizards and snakes retain the eggs, and then at birth the young rupture the membranes and a thin-walled shell. The snake *Coronella austriaca* has this mode of reproduction (sometimes referred to as ovoviviparous). Most lizards and snakes, however, fall into one of two categories: oviparous or viviparous. The distinction is not a fundamental one but the ideas and ecological considerations regarding viviparity are of considerable interest.

Viviparity has evolved only among the Squamata, and in snakes at least probably occurred very early in their evolution. One often-mentioned observation is the apparent relationship between cold environments and viviparity. That is, in cool temperate climates it would seem advantageous for lizards and snakes to retain the eggs and, by basking, to maximize the temperature for the development of the young. In a thorough literature review and excellent synthesis of data by Tinkle and Gibbons (1977), information on altitudinal and latitudinal distribution of lizards and snakes does support the observation that the proportion of viviparous species in the total reptile fauna increases at higher altitudes or higher latitudes. The idea that viviparity is an adaptation to cold is however viewed with suspicion by Tinkle and Gibbons. They offer instead an interesting thesis which considers not only the mode of reproduction but also the fecundity of the lizards and snakes. Evolution of viviparity seems to occur mostly in those environments in which breeding seasons restrict most reptiles to a single brood per year and in which conditions favourable for the development of the young are relatively variable. In regions with less climatic variation, viviparous forms may be at a disadvantage because of a restriction of fecundity. Tinkle and Gibbons conclude that these considerations seem to explain the greater abundance of viviparous species in the temperate zones compared to the tropical regions. Perhaps it is more meaningful to say that this explains the greater proportion of oviparous species in the tropical regions and the relative rarity of multiple broods in temperate climatic regions.

A number of types of placentation has been described for lizards and a few snakes. The lizard *Lacerta vivipara* has an extremely primitive type of placentation (Bellairs, 1971) which permits little transfer of substances other than water and gases. A condition where there is a reduction or loss of shell membranes so that maternal and embryo blood vessels are in close proximity has been found in the New Zealand viviparous gecko *Hoplo-*

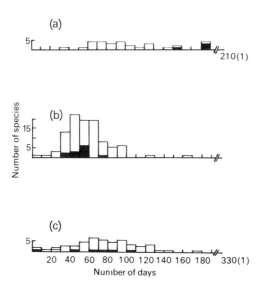

Figure 4.3 Incubation and gestation times of oviparous and viviparous lizards and snakes. (a) viviparous squamates from tropical regions (shaded) and temperate regions (unshaded). (b) oviparous temperate squamates with egg protecting species indicated by shading. (c) oviparous tropical squamates. Redrawn from Tinkle, D. W. and Gibbons, J. W. (1977) *Misc. Publs. Mus. Zool. Univ. Mich.*, **154**, 55 pp.

dactylus, in some skinks, and in some Australian nocturnal elapid snakes of the genus *Denisonia*. One advanced type, the chorio-allantoic placenta, occurs in the skink *Chalcides chalcides* and also in the Australian lygosomids *Lygosoma weekesae* and *Lygosoma entrecasteauxi*.

The time taken for gestation and for incubation is obviously an important aspect of reptile reproductive ecology. Tinkle and Gibbons (1977) have assembled a large sample of gestation and incubation times for both tropical and temperate reptiles (Figure 4.3). No evidence was found for more rapid development times in either tropical oviparous or viviparous species compared to temperate species. However, variation in gestation appears to be greater in oviparous tropical species than in temperate species.

Parthenogenesis (development of a new individual from an unfertilized egg) requires the production of a diploid ovum and is relatively uncommon in vertebrates, but is known to occur successfully in several lacertids, teiids, and in at least one species of each of the families Gekkonidae, Xantusiidae, Agamidae, and Chamaeleontidae. In all cases examined it usually takes the form of thelytoky, that is the production of females from unfertilized eggs. For example Darevsky (1966) has reported natural parthenogenesis in a polymorphic group of Caucasian rock lizards, related to *Lacerta saxicola*, where populations consisted of females with "rare" males. In North America about ten currently recognized species of *Cnemidophorus* (whiptail lizards) are thought to be parthenogenetic. The majority are allotriploids (N = 69) and modified allotriploids (3n = ca. 69) with only two species being allodiploid. In the case of *Cnemidophorus uniparens*, Cuellar (1971) has shown that there is a premeiotic doubling of the chromosomes (endomitosis) followed by an apparently normal meiosis with the diploid (or in some races, triploid) number of bivalents giving rise to an egg nucleus with the parental chromosome number. The same author suggested that genetic modifiers first accumulate to cause endomitosis and parthenogenetic development, giving rise to an autodiploid race. Hybridization between such a race and males from a different sexual species could then give rise to a triploid race, and the modifiers already present in the diploid would ensure the parthenogenetic reproduction of this race. Wright and Lowe (1968) examined the habitats of the parthenogenic *Cnemidophorus* and found that it is widely distributed within habitats that appear unavailable to the bisexual species. It was concluded that the availability of such habitats to newly generated alloploid parthenoforms is significant in the success or failure of the newly constituted genetic combinations produced originally by hybridization.

4.5 Fertilization and development

Fertilization in all reptiles is internal. In many species sperm transfer (copulation) occurs during the spring and is followed almost immediately by fertilization and embryonic development. However, some reptiles are known to mate in the autumn, such as the Australian skink *Hemiergis peronii*, which stores sperm in the oviducts during the winter. It is thought that this sequence is selectively adaptive. Females of this species ovulate early in the following spring and subsequently the young are born early in the summer. This then gives the young more time in which to feed and grow before the winter.

Viability of reptile sperm is generally greater than in most vertebrates and in some species the sperm (after insemination) can survive for many months: e.g., three months in female *Thamnophis sirtalis*. The female box turtle (*Terrapene carolina*) has been reported to lay fertilized eggs up to four years after separation from the male. Delayed fertilization occurs in the Chelonia and in the Squamata, but seminal receptacles occur only in the latter. Sperm storage has obvious advantages and almost certainly contributes towards increased fecundity by eliminating the sometimes complex process of locating a mate.

The formation of a mating plug in some mammals and in insects is well known but only more recently has this phenomenon been described for reptiles. In 1975 Devine reported the discovery of copulatory plugs in the cloacae of female garter snakes (*Thamnophis* sp.). It seems that ejaculation of sperm is followed by a stream of intact sexual segment secretion granules, which precipitates to form a plug matrix. The function of the plugs could be to retain the sperm (advantageous for the female) but it seems more likely that competition amongst males has been important in evolution of copulatory plugs in snakes.

Embryonic development commences with the fertilization of the egg, and owing to the large inert yolk mass the white germinal disc or blastoderm (Figure 4.4), resulting from early cell division, is quite small (Pasteels, 1970). This stage marks the start of gestation (embryonic development within the female reproductive tract) which in some species is followed by laying and incubation. During gastrulation, the single layer of cells making up the blastoderm gives rise to three layers of cells: ectoderm, mesoderm and endoderm. Following the formation of these three germinal layers there begins the process of organ formation, and then early stages in structural development result in the neurula. Tiny networks of blood vessels appear round the embryo at an early stage and by the time the

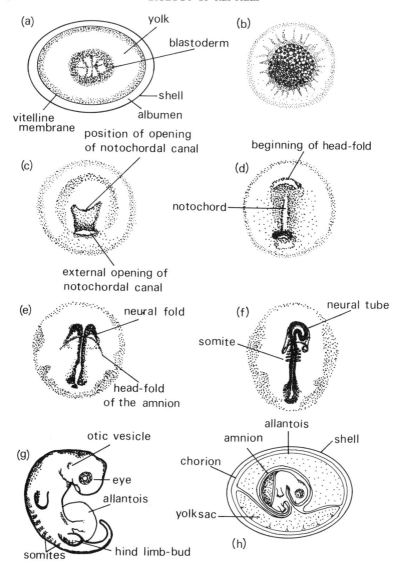

Figure 4.4 Diagrams showing stages in the development of a tortoise. (*a*) and (*h*) are not drawn to the same scale as (*b*)–(*g*). Drawings based on photographs in Yntema, C. L. (1968) *J. Morph.*, **125**, 219–252. (*a*) whole egg with early cleavage (8 cell stage). (*b*) late blastoderm. (*c*) young gastrula. (*d*) very late gastrula. (*e*) showing neural folds. (*f*) 5–6 somite stage. (*g*) formation of limb buds. (*h*) whole egg showing the membranes.

circulatory system is well formed, there is a large number of somites and limb rudiments have also formed (Figure 4.4). In reptiles, as in birds, the endoderm gradually surrounds the yolk, but of more importance is the development of the three extra-embryonic membranes in addition to the yolk sac. The amnion and the chorion develop together as upward-projecting folds and eventually close over the dorsal surface of the embryo. The allantois is a large sac, formed ventrally from the area at the end of the gut, and as the kidneys of the embryo begin to function early in gestation, the allantoic cavity acts as an embryonic bladder. The chorionic and allantoic membranes combined aid the transfer of gases between the porous shell and the blood vessels in the allantoic wall.

At a stage when the embryo lies on its left side, the number of somites has greatly increased, limb rudiments are easily seen and there is also a distinct tail process. In limbless reptiles, there are mechanisms involved in the early morphogenesis of the limbs followed in some cases by retrogression of the limb buds. On hatching, the features of the integument are easily distinguished and the embryo is now recognizable as a miniature adult. An egg tooth is present in lizards and snakes (chelonians and crocodilians have an egg-caruncle) which is used to cut the shell and so aid the hatching process. Tables of normal development have been prepared for the crocodilian *Alligator mississippiensis* (Reese, 1915), for the lizard *Lacerta vivipara* (Dufaure and Hubert, 1961), the snake *Thamnophis sirtalis* (Zehr, 1962) and the turtle *Chelydra serpentina* (Yntema, 1968).

4.6 Reproductive costs, strategies and effort

It is predictable that a female reptile, while gravid, will have a diminished chance of survival. Some species when gravid have a diminished mobility, making them less able to escape from predators. The females of some species, as well as being temporarily less active, will increase their basking time (to promote development) and this behaviour could be expected to increase vulnerability to predation. Others tend to reduce the time normally spent foraging, and so a gravid female which opts to feed less would be using stored energy reserves and could therefore be transposing the energy cost of growth to the cost of producing young.

Each reptile will have evolved a strategy whereby the costs of reproduction are balanced against profits in terms of future gains, that is the fecundity of that particular species. Optimum partitioning of available energy resources between maintenance, growth, and reproduction is important for all species. There are few good studies of reproductive energy costs, and Shine's (1980) field and laboratory data are particularly useful in this context. In six species of Australian scincid lizards, he was able to show that gravid females are more vulnerable to predation than are non-gravid females because they move slowly and tend to bask for prolonged periods. From an extensive review of published literature he concluded that reproductive costs vary widely amongst species and that trade-offs between fecundity and survival are likely to be the main evolutionary determinants of optimum levels of reproductive effort.

It is apparent that there is considerable variation between reptile species in the size of clutch or number of young, age at which maturity is reached, mode of reproduction, and in the nature of the reproductive cycle. Even within one group such as the lacertids there is variation and it is useful to try and identify general patterns of reproductive strategies. In 1970 Tinkle *et al.* identified two principal reproductive strategies for lizards from comparisons of mean clutch size, mean clutches per year, mean age at sexual maturity and related aspects of reproduction. The two strategies identified were (1) early maturing, multiple brooded, and (2) late maturing, single brooded. From an examination of published research on 88 species (embracing eight families) they concluded that, for the early-maturing group, (1) oviparity is the most common mode of reproduction, (2) most are multiple brooded, (3) mean clutch size is significantly smaller than in the other group, (4) more of the variance in clutch size between species is accounted for by consideration of size and of age at first breeding, (5) they are smaller-bodied at maturity, and (6) their distribution tends to tropical and temperate as opposed to the primarily temperate distribution of the second group.

Reproductive strategies are of course closely linked to the concept of the relative nature of r- and K-selection and the r–K continuum. An "r-strategy" refers to species' characteristics such as a high maximum natural rate of increase, sexual maturity reached at an early age, large clutch size, small body size and a short life span, all of which would seem to have evolved in seasonal or unpredictable climates. A K-strategy includes characteristics such as a low maximum rate of increase, delayed repro-duction, small clutch size, large body size, and a long life span, all of which would seem to have evolved in more stable environments. A consideration of reptilian reproductive strategies in this light provides a basis for stimulating and useful discussions, and it should be possible to conclude from species characteristics whether life histories approach an r-strategy or a K-strategy. For example, from Andrews and Rand's (1974) study of *Anolis* lizards (all species lay a clutch of a single egg) it seems that clutch size is small in tropical lizards: this is not to permit larger eggs but to increase fecundity. They suggested that climatic considerations alone explain the selection pressure for lizards with a large clutch size in areas with short and well-defined breeding seasons. That is, in relatively equable tropical habitats, short-term fluctuations in rainfall favour genotypes that are opportunistic reproducers, and relatively high predation intensity favours r-selected life history patterns.

The concept of reproductive effort has long been important for evolutionary ecologists but there is some debate as to how reproductive effort (RE) can best be calculated. A generally accepted definition, based on suggestions made by Williams (1966), is that RE is the total amount of energy and time available to organisms that goes into reproductive related activities including mating, additional costs associated with carrying eggs, egg and shell production, and care of the young. Simple but useful estimates of RE for reptiles have been based on the ratio of clutch weight to body weight. The ratio of clutch weight to body weight in lizards ranges from about 0.1 to 0.4. Avery (1975) has calculated a value of 0.4 for the cool temperate lizard *Lacerta vivipara*. Although this value is comparatively high, Avery noted that the production of a clutch of eggs by *L. vivipara* does not result in the same metabolic drain on the female as is found in many species of fish.

An alternative estimate of RE may be based on the caloric value of the eggs, compared to that of the body. Tinkle and Hadley (1975) measured RE by calculating the ratio of clutch calories to body calories for ten lizard species. Then for three species they considered demographic variations and also calculated maintenance energy budgets from activity and temperature profiles (Table 4.1). Information was available on activity periods and on body temperatures of active lizards at various seasons, and from this it was possible to estimate maintenance energy costs. Oxygen utilized per day was estimated from regression equations relating lizard body size and temperature to oxygen consumption. Energy used in growth in different reproductive age classes was also estimated. For first-time breeders, the authors noted the average gain in weight from that just prior to sexual maturity to that attained during the lizard's first breeding season. The caloric value of this increase in mass was then estimated from caloric measurements made on the bodies of each species. In a similar way, the weight gained between first and second breeding gave an estimate of diversion of calories into growth after the first breeding season. Reproductive effort was calculated to be highest in *Sceloporus graciosus* and lowest in *Sceloporus jarrovi*. The latter, however, shows an increase in RE

Table 4.1   Total energy budgets for different age classes of reproductives in three species of iguanid lizards. Figures are total calories except for proportion shown in parentheses. From Tinkle, D. W. and Hadley, N. F. (1975), *Ecology*, **56**, 427–434.

	First breeders	Second breeders	Third breeders
Sceloporus jarrovi			
Maintenance	21.720	47.040	72.210
Growth	1.877	11.768	7.138
Reproduction	2.530 (0.10)	7.261 (0.11)	11.958 (0.13)
Total	26.127	66.069	91.306
Uta stansburiana			
Maintenance	31.020	34.680	—
Growth	1.156	0.694	—
Reproduction	7.747 (0.19)	8.394 (0.19)	—
Total	39.923	43.768	—
Sceloporus graciosus			
Maintenance	23.040	26.640	30.540
Growth	0.096	0.710	0.480
Reproduction	6.812 (0.23)	8.630 (0.24)	9.517 (0.23)
Total	29.948	35.980	40.537

with age and this seems to be linked to the reproductive cycle, in which mating occurs in autumn and the young are born in the spring. Adults are then able to utilize much of the summer for growth. This species is single-brooded and the effort expended on the single clutch is high. Frequent clutches are laid by *Uta stansburiana*. This is a species which has a high mortality from predation, survivorship of adults to a second breeding season is very low and so therefore selection favours high reproductive effort. The adult life expectancy of *Sceloporus graciosus* is relatively long and sexual maturity is delayed until two years of age. This is advantageous because the older, larger individuals have a higher fecundity and selection should always favour a high RE even in a long-lived species. The long life expectancy and the small difference in survivorship between yearlings and adults of *S. graciosus* suggests that a high RE is accompanied by minimal costs, perhaps (as Tinkle and Hadley suggest) because predation in the population is low, at least compared with *U. stansburiana*.

4.7   Growth and longevity

Studies of reptile growth are scarce, probably because when sexual maturity is reached, rate of growth can be extremely variable. Recognition marking techniques (for a review of methods see Stonehouse, 1978) can provide reliable information on correlations between anatomical and morphological changes, and life history characteristics. But it is often important in ecological research to have a reliable estimate of the animal's actual age. Apart from marking animals at birth (usually difficult or unwise) some anatomical methods have been successfully used to assess individual age of reptiles.

Annulus formation in scutes has proved to be a reliable and successful indicator of age in some species of turtle (Gibbons, 1976), but skeletal annulations (growth rings on bones) have been less useful in determining the age of reptiles. However, recently Castanet (1978), working on lacertilians, has reported some success. Thinner annulations ("lignes d'arrêt de croissance" or LAC) in cross-sections of limb bones are "resting lines" due to slowing down of temperature-dependent growth and these differ structurally from "cementing reversal lines". Castanet reported that the recurrence of the LAC in lacertilians shows an annual regularity and so therefore it would seem that this could be a basis for age determination in lizards.

Mean life expectancy of individuals at different ages can be based on survivorship data but data for reptiles is very rare indeed even for short-lived lizard species. Gibbons (1976) has produced a useful comparison of reptile maximum longevities (based on data from the International Zoo Yearbook) and from this it is possible to make several generalizations. Reptiles as a class do seem to display a slight overall superiority in achieved ages, but the Squamata is not appreciably different from the fishes or amphibians. It is tempting to believe that amongst lizards, the larger forms (which usually have a lower reproductive potential) should have a greater longevity than smaller forms. Turner (1977) has however found no interspecific correlation between survivorship and body size in lizards. Snakes generally live longer than lizards, but the Chelonia and Crocodilia far exceed all other groups of vertebrates in life span potential. Auffenberg and Iverson (1979) have assembled data on growth and longevity of terrestrial tortoises: some species of terrestrial turtles, including emydids, may live longer than 100 years. The biology of ageing in reptiles (and other animals) is discussed in a useful book by Lamb (1977).

CHAPTER FIVE

ECOLOGY: THE PHYSICAL ENVIRONMENT

5.1 Introduction

Living on land, away from the support and shelter of the relatively stable environment provided by water, the reptiles have had to evolve mechanisms for the maintenance of body water balance (homeostasis). From the moment they hatch, leaving their own private "pond" (the egg), adaptations for efficient osmoregulation are paramount to survival. Compared with amphibians, the reptiles have many, but not unique, adaptations for life on land and, in particular, for life in demanding environments such as the desert regions. The most important physical factor in the ecology of reptiles is temperature. Much of their time is devoted to the regulation of their body temperature and maintenance of an optimum body temperature for survival and reproduction. Temperature has also had a powerful influence on the coexistence of reptile species.

5.2 Problems of water balance

In vertebrates, body water occurs extracellularly and intracellularly, separated by semi-permeable cell walls. Paramount to reptile water relations is the maintenance of water balance and maintenance of relatively constant osmotic concentrations, homeostasis being the aim. Like other terrestrial vertebrates, reptiles are able to obtain water from natural sources in the environment, from food and as a product of metabolism: see Dantzler and Holmes (1974) for a specialized account of this topic. There is a lack of evidence to show that terrestrial reptiles use cutaneous absorption as part of their water regulation, and conflicting evidence in the case of amphibious reptiles. Reptiles lose water through their skin, from their respiratory passages and as a product of excretion. But to what extent and by what means can they diminish this loss? For a long time it was accepted that the reptile scale and "dry" skin were the main features associated with water retention. One way to test this idea would, of course, be to compare the water loss of a reptile without scales to that of a reptile which possessed scales. But there remained the problem of obtaining a scale-less reptile. In 1972 Licht and Bennett described a unique form of the gopher snake (*Pituophis melanoleucus catenifer*) which lacked dorsal and lateral body scales. On testing the rates of pulmocutaneous water loss, no difference was observed between the scale-less animal and normal individuals. The reptile scale, from an evolutionary point of view, may therefore have an important role in body temperature regulation, rather than in water balance (Chapter 2). It is of course important to compare water loss from different parts of the reptile body. Schmidt-Nielsen compared the level of evaporation from the reptile skin with the level of evaporation from the respiratory tract, demonstrating very clearly that the contribution made by the skin to the total evaporation was between 66 and 88 %, and always exceeded the respiratory evaporation by a factor of two or more (Schmidt-Nielsen, 1975).

Despite good research on the rate of water loss in reptiles, the different methods used make comparisons difficult. In general, the rate of body water loss varies considerably between different species but will, of course, depend on the ambient temperature, humidity and wind conditions. In general lizards from dry habitats are better able to withstand desiccation

Table 5.1 Evaporative water loss and vital limit (loss in % initial body weight) of five species of lizards at 30°C and 36% r.h. (deprived of food and water). From Munsey, L. D. (1972). *Comp. Biochem. Physiol.*, **43A**, 781–794.

Species	Mean evaporative water loss $(mg\ g^{-1}\ h^{-1}$	Mean vital limit	Habitat
Sceloporus occidentalis	1.34	38.69	Oak woodland — chaparral
Cnemidophorus tigris	0.58	44.91	Mesic and arid
Dipsosaurus dorsalis	0.37	50.23	Arid, semi-arid
Callisaurus draconoides	0.40	45.67	Arid, semi-arid
Uma scoparia	0.41	48.44	Arid

than lizards from mesic habitats. For example, in 1966 Warburg found that Australian agamids conserved water more effectively than Australian skinks or geckos. The rate of body water loss, as recorded under experimental conditions, shows very clearly the inter-specific differences and the relationships to habitat type. Munsey's (1972) study of responses to desiccation of lizards is particularly relevant (Table 5.1). He found that the rate of water loss correlates well with habitat aridity and suggests a general correlation between vital limit and evaporative water loss and the type of habitat.

Some species employ panting as an effective means of cooling. For example *Dipsosaurus dorsalis* (typically occurring in harsh desert regions) uses panting to dissipate heat from oxidative metabolism and to lower its body temperature. Salivation by some species has a similar thermo-regulatory function. Cloudsley-Thompson (1972) found that if the body temperature of *Testudo sulcata* (found in the dry steppes and semi-deserts of central Africa) rises above 40°–41°C, copious salivation takes place through the mouth and nostrils, wetting the head, neck and front of the legs.

The conservation of water is achieved by reptiles using methods common to other taxa. For example, elimination of nitrogen is principally in the form of uric acid (snakes and some chelonians) or in the form of uric acid and ammonia (crocodilians). The tuatara (*Sphenodon*) excretes both urea and uric acid. In the case of marine reptiles, water is scarce and salt abundant, so these animals (as described below) rely on salt-secreting glands. Reptiles can conserve water during elimination of body wastes by absorption of water from both faeces and urine. There is an interesting relationship between the type of habitat and partition of nitrogen in the products of excretion for turtles (Table 5.2). Aquatic species excrete relatively large amounts of ammonia and urea and traces of uric acid, whereas terrestrial species excrete nitrogen mainly as uric acid.

Reabsorption of water in the kidney tubules and the formation of uric acid is a major advantage for life on land. Additional reabsorption can take place in the cloaca of reptiles and faeces are then produced as a semi-solid paste. For example, studies on the xerophilic lizard *Agama stellio* have shown that the cloacal sojourn of uretal urine leads to the absorption of approximately 80% of ureterally excreted NaCl and water (Skadhauge and Duvdevani, 1977). Similar fractions have been reported for other lizard species. As we will see later, different species of reptiles have different body temperatures for normal activity. This being the case, it is perhaps not surprising to discover that in some lizard species, the capacities for

Table 5.2 Partition of nitrogen in the excreta of turtles, given in per cent of total nitrogen excretion. The most aquatic species excretes almost no uric acid, while this compound dominates in the most terrestrial species. From Schmidt-Nielsen, K. (1975) *Animal Physiology*, C.U.P., after Moyle, V. (1949), *Biochem. J.*, **44**, 581–584.

Species	Habitat	Uric acid	Ammonia	Urea	Amino acids	Un-accounted for
Kinosternon subrubrum	Almost wholly aquatic	0.7	24.0	22.9	10.0	40.3
Pelusios derbianus	Almost wholly aquatic	4.5	18.5	24.4	20.6	27.2
Emys orbicularis	Semi-aquatic, feeds on land in marshes	2.5	14.4	47.1	19.7	14.8
Kinixys erosa	Damp places, frequently enters water	4.2	6.1	61.0	13.7	15.2
K. youngii	Drier than above	5.5	6.0	44.0	15.2	26.4
Testudo denticulata	Damp, swampy ground	6.7	6.0	29.1	15.6	32.1
T. graeca	Very dry, almost desert conditions	51.9	4.1	22.3	6.6	4.0
T. elegans	Very dry, almost desert conditions	56.1	6.2	8.5	13.1	12.0

excretion of water and reabsorption of sodium show interspecific differences in thermal dependence related to voluntary (preferred) temperatures. In 1967 Shoemaker *et al.* found that rates of water excretion were much less temperature-dependent in lizards having a low voluntary temperature, but were maximal at about 30°–35°C in the two species examined (*Phyllurus milii* and *Amphibolurus barbatus*).

The physiological basis of water electrolyte balance in reptiles has been examined by many investigators (see Heatwole, 1976, for a review of the literature) and it has been concluded that yet an additional method is required for the elimination of ions if solutes are reabsorbed by active transport from the cloaca. Lizards and marine reptiles have glands which are used for the excretion of salts in highly concentrated forms. The salt-secreting gland of marine turtles is one of the orbital glands, probably the lachrymal. In lizards, salt secretion is by the external nasal gland, which is usually the largest of the nasal glands in reptiles. Salt secretion has been studied in certain lizards; for example, Philpott and Templeton (1964) provide a detailed account of the histology of the salt-excreting gland in *Dipsosaurus*.

The problems of water balance in reptiles are not wholly overcome by physiological processes. Behaviour of the reptile is also important in the conservation of body water and this is seen particularly in desert species (Cloudsley-Thompson, 1972). Shaded rock crevices or burrows are sought by many desert species and there ambient conditions are suited to conserve and reduce body water loss.

5.3 Ectotherms and endotherms

The description of reptiles as "cold blooded" has been used for a long time but this term should be discarded because it is subjective, inaccurate and gives a misleading impression of reptile temperature relations. Reptiles can be said to be *poikilothermic* because they can survive over a relatively wide range of body temperatures, whereas most mammals and birds are *homeothermic* because their body temperatures show little variation when they are active, despite variations in ambient temperature.

The basis for reptile body temperature regulation lies in their use of solar radiation. Whereas birds and mammals generate much of their body heat by oxidative metabolism, reptiles readily absorb heat from their surroundings and this process is aided by their skin, which has good thermal conductance. Largely by behavioural means, but also by using physiological mechanisms, reptiles (as well as fish and amphibians) are able to control the rate of heat exchange between themselves and their immediate surroundings and so therefore we refer to these animals as *ectotherms*. Most mammals and birds are *endothermic* because their body temperature level is determined basically by heat from oxidative metabolism.

In some large reptiles there is the interesting aspect of endothermy (heat derived from its own metabolic activity contributing to the animal's body temperature). Mrosovsky and Pritchard (1971), working on the leatherback turtle (*Dermochelys coriacea*), have found that these reptiles, when offshore from their natural nesting beaches, are commonly 3°C warmer than their environment. That is, the leatherback turtle is sometimes endothermic. Some snakes are at times endothermic. Spasmodic contractions of the body in *Python molurus* have been noted, and it is believed that this generates the heat necessary to maintain an elevated body temperature during brooding. Mierop and Barnard (1976) have reported similar observations on the female python *Molurus bivittatus*, and conclude that since the recorded increased body temperature of their gravid snake (prior to egglaying) cannot be satisfactorily explained by basking, it appears that some endogenous heat production does occur, before and during incubation.

5.4 Body temperature categories

Cowles and Bogert (1944) established the basis of reptile thermoregulatory taxonomy. For each species there is a high and a low body temperature beyond which the animal will die (Figure 5.1). Between these limits there are the critical minimum and the critical maximum temperature: the body temperature at which the animal loses its powers of locomotion. For example if a reptile is slowly cooled and its body temperature is recorded

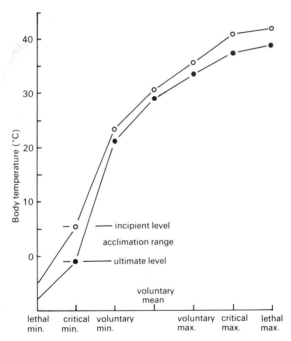

Figure 5.1 Body temperature categories for a hypothetical reptile (typical of a cool temperate species). The incipient and ultimate levels of each category suggest the range of acclimation (or acclimatization) following high temperature and low temperature acclimation.

continuously, the lower body temperature is recorded when the reptile is no longer able to move about. The critical temperatures are sometimes called the ecologically lethal temperatures. In general, reptiles from tropical regions have comparatively high critical minimum temperatures, whereas those from temperate regions have low critical minimum temperatures.

The voluntary maximum temperature (Figure 5.1) is that body temperature at which the reptile will avoid conditions that will further raise its temperature. The voluntary minimum is the body temperature at which the reptile seeks conditions that will raise its body temperature, or conditions which will protect it from very low ambient temperatures. Several methods have been used to determine the voluntary temperatures of reptiles: capture of active reptiles followed by immediate recording of their body temperature; continuous recording of body temperature with the use of telemetry; and continuous recording of body temperatures of captive reptiles maintained in an artificial temperature gradient. All these methods provide data from which it is possible to define the upper and lower limits of body temperature during normal activity: these limits can be equated with the voluntary temperatures. Data collected in this way also make it possible to calculate a mean body temperature for normal activity. The terms "mean preferred body" temperature or "eccritic" temperature are sometimes used in preference to mean voluntary temperature. Highest mean voluntary temperatures occur amongst the Iguanidae and the Agamidae (Figure 5.4) which are common diurnal lizards of deserts and tropical regions.

5.5 Critical temperatures

An endogenous variation has been found for the critical minimum temperature of reptiles (Figure 5.2). This variation, as well as seasonal variations, provides compensation for changes in local temperature conditions. Acclimation (change induced in the laboratory) and acclimatization (change induced by natural conditions) of the critical minimum temperature have, for example, been examined extensively in a group of Australian water skinks (*Sphenomorphus*) and interesting aspects of the critical minimum temperature were discovered (Spellerberg, 1972). One species from south-eastern Australia was known to occur as two colour morphs: one distributed throughout wet sclerophyll forest (cool) and one in dry sclerophyll forest (warm). Having measured the critical minimum temperatures of this species (Figure 5.3) it was possible to

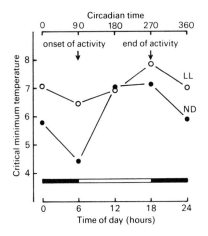

Figure 5.2 Critical minimum temperature data of a lizard (*Lacerta sicula*) as a function of time. ND, animals kept under natural daylight conditions and temperature cycle of 10–33°C. LL, animals kept under constant light intensity (52 lux) and temperature (26°C). From Spellerberg, I. F. and Hoffmann, K. (1972) *Naturwiss.*, **11**, 517–518.

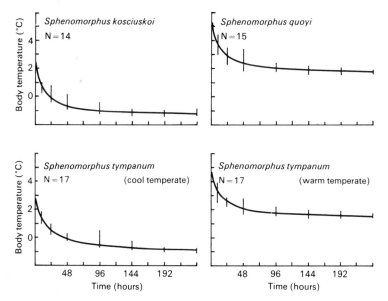

Figure 5.3 Acclimation curves for the critical minimum temperatures of some southeastern Australian reptiles. The vertical line shows the range for each critical minimum determined. N = number of lizards tested.

distinguish not just two forms but two physiological races (almost certainly two different species). The one with a comparatively low critical minimum temperature (2.9°C) occurred in the cool temperate areas and the one with a comparatively high critical minimum temperature (6.1°C) was restricted to the warm temperate areas.

A further species of water skink (*S. kosciuskoi*), restricted to areas of sub-alpine and montane vegetation, had the very low critical minimum temperature of 2.5°C. That was the figure obtained from animals collected in the summer, but it was found that come winter, this species would acclimatize and adjust its critical minimum temperature to the astonishing level of −1.2°C without freezing. During winter these animals were able to move (below the cover of snow) while they were in a supercooled state. The ability of this and other lizard species to supercool (deep body temperature below the freezing point of the animal's blood) is closely linked to the ecology of the species and particularly the winter ecology (Spellerberg, 1972).

In 1980, Greer examined lizard thermal ecology with particular reference to the critical maximum temperatures of Australian reptile species. Taxa from warm interior areas of Australia generally had a mean critical maximum greater than 39.5°C regardless of their behaviour or habitat. Those from the cooler and coastal areas could be divided into two groups: the diurnal surface-dwelling forms generally have a mean critical maximum above 39.5°C; the crepuscular to nocturnal, or cryptozoic to fossorial forms had a mean critical maximum below 39.5°C.

5.6 Voluntary (preferred) temperatures

There are many estimates of reptile voluntary temperatures (Figure 5.4), but few attempts to establish the extent to which reptiles are able to control and regulate their body temperature. Body temperature control in reptiles has both a physiological and a behavioural basis. The physiological basis includes (1) cardiovascular mechanisms including the ability to alter the rate of blood flow; (2) alteration in integument reflectance; and (3) evaporative cooling so that heat is dissipated via the buccal cavity as a consequence of panting.

The ability to control the rate of change of body temperature by physiological means is known to occur in reptiles from several families (see Cloudsley-Thompson, 1971, for a review). This is a mechanism which allows the reptile to extend its period of activity during which its body temperature is held within the voluntary temperature range. A particularly

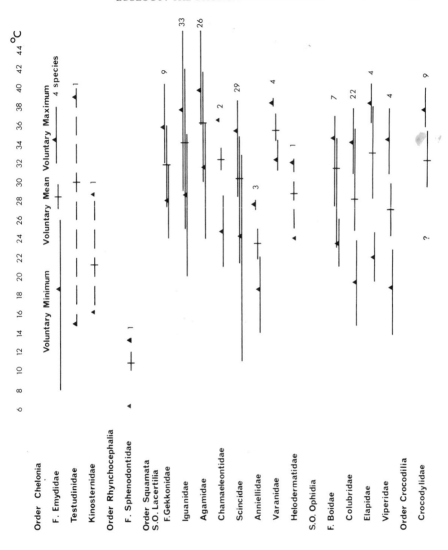

Figure 5.4 Reptile voluntary (preferred) temperatures. Data are combined for each family (number of species noted) and the range of each voluntary minimum, voluntary mean and voluntary maximum is indicated. The mean value is shown by the triangle. Data from numerous sources and cited in Spellerberg, I. F. (1977) *The Herptile*, **11**, 8–37.

interesting example of this was found in a study of the Galapagos marine iguana (*Amblyrhynchus cristatus*). This species spends much time on rocky shores exposed to intense radiation and has a voluntary temperature of about 37°C. The marine iguana feeds on marine algae in relatively cool water and in doing so its body temperature drops by 10° or 15°C. However, the rate at which its body temperature decreases is about half the rate at which it increases when it returns to the warm rocky shore. The basis for this slow cooling and fast heating rate is to be found in cardiovascular mechanisms. Bartholomew and Lasiewski (1965) found that the heart rate at a given temperature was generally more rapid during heating than during cooling. In simple terms, the rate of heat exchange between the animal's deep tissues and the environment will in part depend on the volume of blood flowing between the core and the surface of the animal. It would seem therefore that blood circulation augments heat exchange during heating and diminishes it during cooling. This effect is further increased by peripheral vasodilatation during heating and peripheral vasoconstriction during cooling (Bartholomew, 1968). The literature on reduced heart rates in diving reptiles has been summarized by Pough (1973).

Much has been written about the role of reptile integument colour and how dark-coloured forms should be able to warm more quickly than light-coloured forms. Caution is necessary, however, when thinking in terms of visible colour, because the integument reflectance is a product of skin texture and other variables as well as visible colour. Percent integument reflectance can be measured (Figure 5.5) and from this kind of datum it is possible to show that colour change from light to dark is, in some species and under some circumstances, a factor contributing to net energy gain. Desert species tend to have a high integument reflectance, and in general interspecific differences in reflectance correlate well with the type of habitat. Using the information in Figure 5.5 it has been possible to compare different species and to show that under similar conditions the small, dark-coloured species from high-altitude areas (*Sphenomorphus kosciuskoi*) has a potentially greater rate of heating than the larger light-coloured species from lowland areas (*S. quoyi*). That integument colour has a role in the thermal ecology of reptiles is without doubt, but colour and colour change in reptiles seems to be of greater importance for camouflage and social behaviour.

Behavioural thermoregulation in heliothermic reptiles basically consists of orientation, posturing and shuttling. Of these, orientation to the heat source is probably the least important in determining a reptile's body

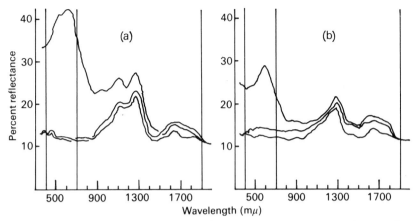

Figure 5.5 Percent integument reflectance of *Sphenomorphus quoyi* (*a*) and *Sphenomorphus kosciuskoi* (*b*). Between 500 and 1500 mμ and in order of decreasing magnitude: ventral surface (25°C); dorsal surface (25°C); dorsal surface (4°C). From Spellerberg (1972) *Oecologia*, **9**, 23–46.

temperature. Some reptiles are largely thigmothermic, obtaining heat by contact with their surroundings. Judicious selection of microhabitats and microclimates is important when a reptile regulates its body temperature, and so reptile species which inhabit cool and cold temperate regions usually make good use of sheltered and sunny areas (Heatwole, 1976).

The thermoregulatory behaviour of desert reptiles has been well researched (Avery, 1979). In many diurnal desert species there is a distinct diel pattern of behaviour, commencing with orientation and posturing, which results in a body temperature suitable for activity. Maintenance of that body temperature is achieved by shuttling, then towards the end of the day there is a return to posturing, followed by return to a burrow for shelter at night. Behavioural thermoregulation in all reptiles is highly effective, and each species has its own particular form of behaviour enabling it to successfully exploit its thermal environment.

There seems no doubt that the daily activity of many reptile species can be correlated with specific limits of body temperature, and that the foraging behaviour of some species occurs when their body temperature is within a narrow range. The extent to which reptiles actively respond to changes in their thermal environment has been debated. Although the behaviour of some reptiles seems to be associated with precise thermo-regulatory ability (Chapter 7), the temperature regulation of some lizards could be said to be no better than a water-filled beer can (Heath, 1964).

A rather curious exception to the general pattern of temperature requirements has been described by Clarke (1973) who examined the temperature responses of three Costa Rican *Anolis* lizards. Two species (*A. cupreus* and *A. intermedius*) were reported to be heliothermic, but a third species (*A. polylepis*) did not bask, and Clarke suggested that as *A. polylepis* were active throughout the day, and the species is behaviourally indifferent across the range of body temperatures recorded (20.9°–29.3°C), then it would be pointless to calculate a mean or preferred body temperature.

Another interesting exception has been found in the case of the desert iguana, *Dipsosaurus dorsalis* (De Witt, 1967). These iguanas exercise control over their body temperature with some precision—De Witt found 95% of body temperatures to be between 33.2°C and 41.8°C. However, a surprising adaptation to desert conditions is shown by this species: in summer, desert iguanas can prolong their activity period by permitting body temperatures to rise above the voluntary maximum, and during territorial fighting behaviour and in the presence of predators, body temperatures rise well above 41.8°C.

5.7   The importance of voluntary temperatures

Many aspects of a reptile's ecology, physiology and neurology can be affected by the animal's body temperature. For example, the rate of digestion by reptiles is largely dependent on body temperature, and a thermophilic response has been reported for several lizard and snake species (that is, following feeding, the reptiles will seek warmth, and an appropriate high body temperature will increase the efficiency of digestion). Skoczylas (1970) described the influence of temperature on gastric digestion in the grass snake (*Natrix natrix*), and found that digestion ceased at 5°C, at 15°C digestion was retarded and sometimes the snake regurgitated undigested food, at 25°C digestion seemed to proceed efficiently, and at 35°C digestion proceeded at a normal or slightly slower rate. Independently (Spellerberg, 1976) it was found that the voluntary minimum for this species is 15°C, the voluntary maximum is 36°C and the mean or average voluntary temperature is 26°C.

The relationship between reptilian reproductive cycles and environmental factors has received a great deal of attention: in particular, the influence of photoperiod (daylength) and body temperature has been closely researched. The importance of voluntary temperatures for lizard reproduction was dramatically demonstrated by Licht (1965) when he exposed specimens of *Urosaurus ornatus*, *Sceloporus virgatus* and *S.*

graciosus to temperatures 1–2°C above their respective voluntary temperature ranges. The lizards suffered marked spermatogenic damage and a decline in appetite and body weight, whereas lizards kept in conditions where they could achieve an average voluntary temperature level were not affected. Continuous exposures even to voluntary temperature levels may be detrimental to both reproductive and somatic tissues: this supports the idea that body temperature cycles are of functional importance.

In 1976 Pough reported that in several species of lizards and snakes, blood oxygen capacity is maximal within the species' activity temperature range (Figure 5.6). The correlation coefficient between the eccritic temperature (mean voluntary) and the temperature giving maximum blood oxygen capacity for all species tested was 0.79 (P < 0.01).

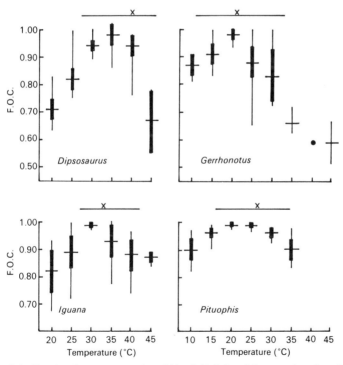

Figure 5.6   Fractional oxygen capacity of blood (F.O.C.) of four species of reptiles as a function of temperature. Vertical line = range, horizontal line = mean, rectangle = 2SE. The line above each graph shows the voluntary temperature range and X indicates the mean voluntary temperature. Redrawn from Pough, F. H. (1976) *Physiol. Zool.*, **49**, 141–151.

Many forms of reptile behaviour have been shown to depend on body temperature levels. For example, in several lizard species the temperature of maximum auditory sensitivity has been found to vary as a function of the natural thermal preference for each species. In 1974, Greenwald reported that the striking and prey capture behaviour of the gopher snake (*Pituophis catenifer affinis*) increased in efficiency as body temperature increased. It was most efficient at 27°C, which was also the average field body temperature for this species as recorded by Greenwald. Thus the average field body temperature is also optimal for success in prey capture.

It is interesting to note that in some localities the voluntary temperatures of congeneric and sympatric species are dissimilar, whereas congeneric and allopatric species have similar voluntary temperatures (Spellerberg, 1972). This has obvious implications for the efficient utilization of thermal resources. Lee's (1980) study of the thermal ecology of the lizard *Anolis sagrei* provides good evidence for the hypothesis that energetic costs are important in controlling the extent to which lizards thermoregulate. In habitats considered to be energetically costly for thermoregulation (i.e. those with patches of sunlight), the mean body temperature of *Anolis sagrei* was 29.2°C, but in open habitats where the costs of thermoregulation were low the mean body temperature was 32.2°C. This supports the idea that where costs are low, lizards thermoregulate more precisely than where costs are high.

It would seem reasonable to suggest that sustained and relatively high body temperature levels have been equally important for reptiles throughout their evolution. It is interesting that the voluntary temperatures for *Sphenodon* are low compared to other reptiles (Figure 5.4). A low voluntary temperature is probably not important to this animal's survival today (many ectothermic organisms function successfully at low temperatures) but it may have been important to the species' survival over thousands of years.

We can but speculate on the body temperature and energy metabolism of extinct reptiles. Living ectotherms and endotherms have different metabolic rates. We can distinguish between the bradymetabolic animals (those with slow rates of chemical change) and the tachymetabolic animals. The latter are the birds and mammals which have a high rate of metabolism and which probably evolved independently from bradymetabolic reptilian ancestors. Despite the suggestion that basic biochemical and central nervous requirements for endothermy may have existed in reptilian ancestors, the evidence for endothermic dinosaurs is conflicting. A high stable body temperature could be maintained by large dinosaurs living in conditions where fluctuations in temperature were small. One suggestion is that large size, with a high heat storage capacity, would result in body temperature stability (Spotila *et al.*, 1973). This mechanism would be an advantage during cool periods, but it could equally well be a disadvantage in warm periods. Cloudsley-Thompson and Butt (1977) have suggested that terrestrial forms as large as even the smallest Cretaceous dinosaurs (with extremely low surface-to-volume ratios) would have suffered from endothermic overheating at ambient temperatures above 35°C, even if their metabolic rates were no higher than that of a tortoise. Perhaps it was the heat and not the cold that brought about the extinction of the dinosaurs.

5.8 Body temperature and energy metabolism

When considering energy metabolism of ectothermic organisms we usually refer to the standard metabolic rate: this is the metabolism of an ectotherm at a given body temperature where the animal is resting and is in a post-absorptive state. For birds and mammals, the stable minimal rate of energy metabolism under similar conditions is usually referred to as the basal metabolic rate. As would be expected, the standard metabolic rate of reptiles usually increases with temperature, behaving like a biochemical system *in vitro* with a doubling of oxygen consumption with each 10

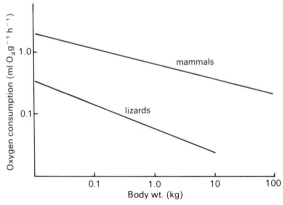

Figure 5.7 Log-log plot of oxygen consumption of mammals and lizards against body weight. Data for lizards from Bartholomew, G. A. and Tucker, V. A. (1964) *Physiol. Zool.*, **37**, 341–354. Equation for calculating metabolic rate of lizards from their body weight: $M = 0.82w^{0.62}$.

centigrade degree increase in temperature. Despite the long-standing separation of the surviving reptilian lines and their ecological diversity, the standard or resting metabolism appears to have been a conservative feature. Since this does not appear to vary significantly, it is possible to establish the relation between oxygen consumption at a given temperature and the body weight of the animal (Figure 5.7). It is notable that the standard metabolic rate of reptiles (in this case lizards) is markedly below that of endothermic animals of comparable size.

A useful concept in animal energetics concerned with the understanding of energy metabolism in an ecological context, is metabolic "scope for activity". This is the capacity of the animal for activity, expressed as a difference between the resting metabolic rate and that which occurs when the animal is fully active. It is an indication of the extent to which a particular animal can increase its activity. Some reptiles, such as *Tiliqua nigrolutea* (an Australian blue-tongued skink), are slow-moving and are not able to greatly increase their locomotion when approached by a predator; others, such as some of the agamids, will rapidly and suddenly resort to bipedal locomotion (be it briefly) to escape predators. Different species therefore have different strategies for feeding and for escape behaviour and this can in some instances be linked to their metabolic scope. For example the standard metabolism of a 700 g *Varanus* at 37°C is $0.13 \, \text{cm}^3 \, \text{O}_2 \, \text{g}^{-1} \, \text{h}^{-1}$. The maximum sustained metabolic rate in *Varanus* exceeds $1.0 \, \text{cm}^3 \, \text{O}_2 \, \text{g}^{-1} \, \text{h}^{-1}$ which surpasses the basal rate of a mammal by about 30% (Bartholomew, 1968). This is an extreme case but it does illustrate the concept of metabolic scope, and we could consider these results as bridging a metabolic gap between reptiles and mammals.

During periods of high energy demand, the aerobic metabolism of reptiles may be supplemented by anaerobic processes which are primarily based on the degradation of glycogen or glucose to lactic acid. Reptiles, with their limited capacity for oxygen transport, appear extensively reliant on, and tolerant of, energy generation by lactate production. This is partly explained by the low thermal dependence of anaerobic metabolism which makes it an ideal system for energy mobilization in ectotherms, contrasted with aerobic metabolism which is strongly temperature-dependent. The amount of energy obtained anaerobically is found from the total lactate production of animals (in mg lactate per g body weight) derived from the levels determined from whole animal homogenates: blood lactate levels alone cannot be used, due to the dynamic and compartmentalized nature of the production and metabolism of lactate. Anaerobic scope is calculated from the difference in lactate levels between active and resting animals, and

Table 5.3 Aerobic and anaerobic scope contribution to metabolic scope. Expressed as μ moles ATP per g body weight and also shown as % of total scope. * = mean voluntary temperature. From Bennett, A. F. and Gleeson, T. T. (1976), *Physiol. Zool.*, **49**, 65–76.

Species	Average weight of sample	Body temp. °C	Aerobic scope	Anaerobic scope	Total scope
Sceloporus	13.1 g	20	4.1–19%	17.9–81%	21.9
occidentalis		25	7.6–31%	17.1–69%	24.7
		30	10.8–21%	28.8–79%	39.6
		35*	12.7–34%	25.3–66%	38.0
		40	12.1–38%	19.6–62%	31.7
Dipsosaurus	35 g	25	4.6–20%	18.0–80%	22.6
dorsalis		30	7.7–27%	20.7–73%	28.4
		35	14.5–40%	21.5–60%	36.0
		40*	21.9–42%	30.2–58%	52.1
		45	12.5–36%	22.3–64%	34.8

a comparison with aerobic scope can be made by conversion of both to equivalent amounts of ATP (Table 5.3).

The adaptations of diving reptiles make a useful comparison with those of terrestrial reptiles. Some aquatic chelonians can for example dive for long periods of time and tolerate elevated blood P_{CO_2}, increased acidity, and reduced blood P_{O_2}. Although anaerobic glycolysis provides metabolic energy during prolonged anoxia, the continuous dependence on oxygen by certain vital organs seems not to be a limiting factor in diving turtles (Jackson, 1979). The duration of a dive depends upon the ability to support vital processes by anaerobic metabolism, which in turn depends upon the level of activity and the body temperature. A further adaptive modification for diving seems to be the ability to extract oxygen from water. The skin of turtles is not generally adapted for absorbing oxygen from water, yet absorption does occur in some species (Girgis, 1961).

Oxygen consumption in reptiles has been shown to be a direct exponential function of temperature, with Q_{10} values between two and three. However, the rate-temperature curves for some species show temperature-dependent changes and it is also possible to show the effects of acclimation or acclimatization to different temperature regimes. This temperature-dependent variation is thought to involve multiple forms of specific enzymes or isoenzymes. The acclimation of reptiles to specific experimental test temperatures generates an "acclimated curve" demonstrating time-dependent compensation. In contrast, the "acute curve" is obtained when the reptile is exposed to different temperatures without

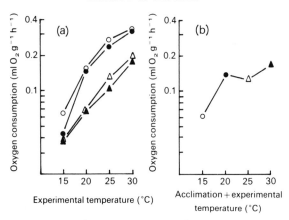

Figure 5.8 (*a*) Acutely determined oxygen consumption rate-temperature curves of four thermal acclimation groups of *Sceloporus olivaceus*: 15°C (○), 20°C (●), 25°C (△) and 30°C (▲). (*b*) Acclimation oxygen consumption rate-temperature curve of four acclimation groups of *S. olivaceus*: 15°C (○), 20°C (●), 25°C (△) and 30°C (▲). Redrawn from Dutton, R. H. and Fitzpatrick, L. C. (1975) *Comp. Biochem. Physiol.*, **51**A, 309–318.

prior acclimation to each test temperature. In 1975, Dutton and Fitzpatrick reported rate temperature curves for *Sceloporus olivaceus* which, for two weeks, had been acclimated to various temperatures and photoperiods, with reduced photoperiods at the lower acclimation temperatures (Figure 5.8). The cold-acclimated groups (15°C and 20°C) showed partial time-dependent compensation relative to the warm-acclimated animals, and these differences were used to construct the acclimated curve (Figure 5.8*b*). The acute rate-temperature curves in Figure 5.8 show that this species is capable of metabolic compensation. Lizards that lower their metabolic rate at high temperatures presumably benefit from conservation of energy, particularly when active during the day.

In 1971, Aleksiuk reported temperature-dependent shifts in the metabolism of the cool temperate snake *Thamnophis sirtalis parietalis*. In this case, the rate-temperature curve for each individual tested was determined during the course of one day (Figure 5.9). Compared with a subtropical form there was a marked shift in the level of oxygen consumption of the cool temperate form at about 15°C. It was concluded that this represents an instantaneous temperature-dependent mechanism of temperature compensation. It is advantageous for those species inhabiting cold regions to have some form of instantaneous compensation to offset the otherwise depressive effects of low temperature on metabolism.

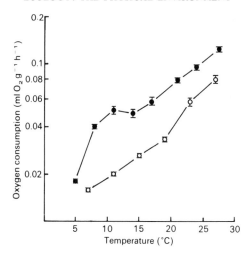

Figure 5.9 Oxygen consumption rate-temperature curve for cool temperate (○) and subtropical (●) representatives of the snake *Thamnophis sirtalis*. Brackets indicate SD of the means. Redrawn from Aleksiuk, M. (1971) *Comp. Biochem. Physiol.*, **39A**, 495–503.

More recent evidence for physiological adjustments to cold and genotypically mediated adaptation to climate has been described by Davies and Bennett (1981). Rate-temperature curves (derived from acute resting oxygen consumption rates) were calculated for juvenile *Natrix natrix helvetica* (cool temperate) and juvenile *Natrix maura* (warm temperate). Oxygen consumption rates of *N. natrix* were found to be significantly higher at each of the five test temperatures (5–27°C) than those of *N. maura*. Values for the cool temperate species represent a compensatory adjustment of metabolism that allows the species to maintain comparatively high metabolic rates at low temperatures. Where rate-temperature curves differ in this way, it is possible to identify a number of patterns in the type of shift. Prosser's (1958) classification of patterns of compensatory changes in rate-temperature curves includes two basic types. In the translation type the curve shifts to the left and up, or to the right and down. In the rotation type, the slope of the rate-temperature curve for cool temperate animals may be different to that of warm temperate animals, with the result that they cross at some midpoint on the temperature gradient. Translation shifts of the kind found for juvenile natricine snakes are well known for ectothermic animals.

A further and particularly interesting aspect of rate-temperature curves is that differences resulting are sometimes greater at lower temperatures than at higher temperatures. Patterson and Davies (1978) recorded rates of oxygen consumption at different temperatures for different seasonal acclimation groups of four lizard species, *Podarcis hispanica, Psammodromus hispanicus, Lacerta vivipara* and *Anguis fragilis*. In the case of *Podarcis hispanica* and *Psammodromus hispanicus* it was found that low temperature metabolic rates are lowest in winter and in spring. In the region where these species originate, it is at these seasons that the longest periods of adverse weather, when the lizards cannot be active, occur. In the case of *Lacerta vivipara* and *Anguis fragilis*, low temperature metabolism is less in autumn than in spring or summer; this has been suggested as a mechanism for reducing low temperature energy expenditure in cool temperate animals entering, or about to enter, winter inactivity. The common pattern of acclimation of oxygen consumption in temperate reptiles is determined by considerations of low temperature energy conservation (Patterson and Davies, 1978).

5.9 Winter dormancy

Hibernation, an adaptation to seasonal cold, occurs in some small mammals. Periodic arousal for short intervals of time is a characteristic of hibernating mammals, but there are a number of physiological differences between seasonally inactive mammals and reptiles. The distinction between hibernation (seasonal torpor associated with cold), and winter dormancy in reptiles, can be appreciated when the different patterns of adaptive hypothermia are considered. For example, adaptive hypothermia in endotherms includes daily torpor and seasonal torpor; the latter includes hibernation and aestivation (dormancy associated with warm and dry conditions). Seasonal torpor or winter dormancy in reptiles has sometimes been termed brummation so as to distinguish it from hibernation. The ecology of winter dormancy in reptiles has received little attention and the underlying mechanisms are largely unknown. Entry into the dormant state seems to be triggered by temperature levels and light cycles, but nothing is known about the mechanisms involved. The structure and physical conditions of wintering sites have been well described for several species: in general the wintering site must afford protection from conditions which would cause the reptile's body temperature to fall below the critical temperature. Large wintering aggregations of reptiles are not uncommon, and the explanation has been debated. Individuals packed closely together could possibly benefit from conservation of heat energy; a further suggestion is that aggregations facilitate early mating behaviour because many individuals emerge at about the same time.

Studies on reptile metabolism during the winter non-active period have, in some instances, provided evidence for adaptive alterations at the "whole organism" level of energy metabolism. Other studies of the physiology of reptiles have shown not only that caudal fat is utilized by dormant reptiles, but that species at high altitudes have particularly large fat reserves. From results of histochemical investigation, Pollock and MacAvoy (1978) suggest that energy requirements of skeletal muscle in dormant lizards are largely met by increased lipid metabolism (Chapter 2).

CHAPTER SIX

ECOLOGY: THE BIOTIC ENVIRONMENT

6.1 Introduction

Organisms interact with their biotic environment as well as interacting with their physical and chemical surroundings. Relationships with other organisms of the same species primarily affect population size, recruitment, mortality and dispersion. Interactions with other species affect the structure of the community in which the organism is found. There are few good estimates of reptile population size and population density, and the best examples come from the Squamata. The estimates of home range size and territory size are also limited to a few groups. This lack of information is regrettable because the home range or territory plays an important role in the way an organism interacts with its environment. Two factors closely related to intraspecific variation in population density are food abundance and food availability. They are also central to the analysis of community structure, and in the development of ideas on the way sympatric species partition their resources. Despite the few detailed studies on reptile population dynamics, research on reptiles has contributed much to recent debates on the concept of niche. Some aspects of this very important work are reviewed here.

6.2 Population size and population density

It is a first basic step in field ecology to estimate numbers of individuals because a knowledge of population size is necessary before the structure and dynamics of a community can be understood. For a rare species which is relatively restricted to a defined area, it is comparatively easy to measure the population size by counting individuals (within a short space of time).

It is usual, however, to find that estimates of reptile population size require perhaps many weeks, months or years to complete. In monitoring exercises, and for determining a measure of relative abundance, it is sometimes useful to record periodically numbers of newly captured individuals and numbers of previously marked individuals. The effects of mortality and dispersal over a long time period make estimates of relative abundance somewhat limited in value. All capture-mark-recapture methods are based on several assumptions and all have their limitations. However, one relatively useful method has been suggested by Turner (1977). He proposed that the following equation (based on several samples) could be used as a basis for estimating the abundance and density of reptiles:

$$\hat{P} = a(n-1)(r-1)$$

where $\hat{P}$ = is population estimation
       a = number marked in first sample
       r = number marked animals recaptured.

The variance of $\hat{P}$ (described by Bailey, 1952) could be estimated as follows:

$$\text{Var}\,(\hat{P}) = \frac{a^2(n+1)(n-r)}{(r+1)^2(r+2)}$$

This equation is but one of a large family of Lincoln Index-based equations and is not appropriate to all reptile species. The equation(s) chosen will depend on the circumstances and on the ecological and behavioural characteristics unique to the species under study.

A measure of population size provides a basis for further analysis of populations but even more valuable is a measure of population density. Estimates of population density are particularly relevant to an understanding of how the organism exploits its resources. It is of course necessary to determine the area occupied by the population if the density of the population is to be calculated: the extent of the area occupied has often proved difficult to delineate. Indexes of density have however been based on repeated counts in quadrats of various sizes but this method should be tested against measures of known densities.

Intraspecific variation in population density is not unusual (Heatwole, 1976). The density of tortoise populations will, for example, vary with the nature of the habitat, and may change, particularly in the case of marine species, on a seasonal basis as a result of migratory and nesting behaviour. Ironically there are few population studies of marine turtles, yet many of them have been exploited to the extent that some are vulnerable or endangered, for example *Chelonia mydas* (green turtle), *Eretmochelys imbricata* (hawksbill), *Lepidochelys* (Radley's), and *Dermochelys cariacea* (leatherback). Few estimates of population density and population size are available for freshwater and terrestrial species. Moll and Legler (1971) estimated the population density of *Pseudemys scripta* in Panama as 26–31 per ha and reported densities of *Chrysemys picta* as 67–94 per ha. Plummer (1977) estimated about 1900 *Trionyx muticus* to be within a 1.5 km section of a Kansas river and found that there was a great weekly variability which was possibly caused by movement of individuals over several km. Stickel's research (1978) on box turtle (*Terrapene carolina*) populations over three decades stands out as one of the few detailed long-term studies. She found that there was a pronounced decline in population size, particularly between 1965 and 1975 (the last decade), which probably resulted from disproportionate losses of females and failure of recruitment of young.

In 1971 Grubb reported a population of about 100 000 *Geochelone gigantea* on Aldabra Atoll, with a density of about 30 km^{-2} on the plantin, but higher densities in woodland. As in the case of many other terrestrial species, the population density is profoundly affected by the availability of shade.

Much of the data available for lizard population size and population density is ecologically meaningful and reliable, partly because populations of many species tend to remain in well-defined areas and can be observed relatively easily. In 1977 Turner summarized information relating to lizard densities, particularly those based on capture-recapture estimates (Figure 6.1). It is particularly interesting to see that the highest population densities are for anoles in highly productive tropical areas and where the habitat has a particularly complex structure. Population density of some anole species changes on a seasonal basis in response to strong seasonal changes in the tropical environment. Spatial differences in population density of other lizard species results from differences in habitat quality. Bustard's (1971) two-year field study of the Australian gecko *Oedura ocellata* resulted in data showing that variation in population density was caused by availability of homesites (shelter under loose bark).

Whereas estimates of lizard population size and densities seem to be ecologically meaningful, those for snakes are difficult to interpret. Anyone who has worked on the ecology of snakes will appreciate that some are highly vagile and that, despite strenuous efforts, it is sometimes very difficult to locate and mark a good proportion of the population. Snakes occupying winter dens or emerging from wintering sites have, in some

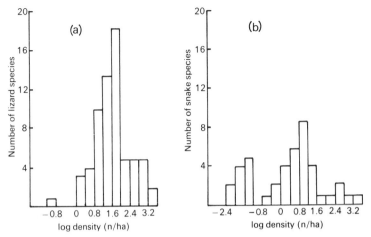

Figure 6.1   The range and distribution of estimated densities of lizards (*a*) and snakes (*b*).
Redrawn from Turner, F. B. (1977) in Gans, C. and Tinkle, D. W., *Biology of the Reptilia*, Vol.
17, Academic Press, pp. 157–264.

instances, provided material for good estimates of population size (up to
95 %) but this is exceptional in population studies of snakes. There are
therefore severe difficulties in interpreting data from estimates of snake
populations, and snake densities are generally lower than is usually
reported—the snake population densities shown in Figure 6.1 are based
mainly on Turner's very careful review and show densities often much
lower than sometimes reported in research reports. Here the lowest density
is for a boid and the highest estimated densities are for the colubrids
Thamnophis, Carphophis and *Coluber*.

   In some locations, the behaviour and the distribution of crocodilians
along water courses has enabled direct counts and easy estimates of
population density, particularly where daily activity and movements have
been studied. For example, Cott's (1961) work on the Nile crocodile
(*Crocodylus niloticus*) in Uganda and Northern Rhodesia showed that this
species (like many others) is nocturnally aquatic. Although little is known
about local movements, the Nile crocodile does follow floodwaters that
spread over the plains with the result that some animals are distributed
well away from permanent water. Numbers of Nile crocodiles per km of
river or shore have been recorded—e.g. estimates from localities in
Uganda range from 0.06 animals per km for the east shore of Lake Albert
to 26.27 for the Victoria Nile below the Murchison Falls (Turner, 1977).

6.3   Home range and territory

The extent to which an animal moves about (vagility) and the spacing of
the individuals within a population (dispersion) can usefully be examined
by recording the home range or the territory size. Methods of estimating
the home range size do contain biologically unrealistic assumptions;
nevertheless they provide an index of movement and spacing. A home
range is the area over which an animal moves in pursuit of its normal
activities. A territory, although it need not be an exclusive area, is an area
defended by an animal against individuals of the same species: territorial
behaviour needs to be identified before the species could be said to possess
a territory. Home ranges are calculated from recapture points and two
common methods are those using recapture radii and those using polygon
techniques. Home ranges are defined statistically in terms of decreasing
probability of capture from the geometric centre of the capture points, but
if the home range lacks circular symmetry, then methods based on capture
radii will suffer large biases. Many lizard home ranges are not circular
(some are linear in shape), and therefore it has been important to devise a
method which does not assume a circular home range. In 1969 Jennrich
and Turner reviewed popular methods for the estimation of home range,
and developed a method based on the determination of the covariance
matrix of the capture points which does not assume a circular home range,
in which outermost points are connected to form the smallest possible
convex polygon. Correction factors, from simulated distribution of capture
points, have been calculated which adjust the convex polygon home range
according to the number of recaptures (see Table 2 in Jennrich and Turner,
1969).

There is little evidence to suggest that chelonians show territorial
behaviour but a few, including slider turtles (*Pseudemys*), box turtles
(*Terrapene*) and the Texas tortoise (*Gopherus belandiere*), do have home
ranges. The evidence for home ranges amongst the giant tortoises on the
Galapagos Islands (*Geochelone elephantopus*) and on the island atoll of
Aldabra (*G. gigantea*) is conflicting. The latter species has a well-marked
cycle of activity, feeding during the early morning and the late evening.
Some individuals wander randomly over about 7–8 km within two-month
periods of time while others do not seem to have a recognizable home
range.

The only extensive knowledge available on vagility and spacing patterns
in reptiles comes from studies on lizards: some results from research on
one family, Iguanidae, deserve a special mention. Iguanids tend to be

diurnal, terrestrial or arboreal, and insectivorous. Their home ranges are from about 53 m^{-2} to about 5656 m^{-2}. In general, male iguanids tend to be territorial and exhibit aggressive behaviour: one species reported not to be territorial is *Anolis agassizi* (Stamps, 1977). Ferner's (1974) study of *Sceloporus undulatus erythrocheilus* illustrates some of the more interesting aspects of home ranges in this family. He found that home ranges of males (826 m^2) were 2–3 times as large as those of females (363 m^2) reflecting greater activity in males. It is not unusual amongst iguanid lizards for more than one female to be in the home range of territory of a male, and during the breeding season females may vigorously defend a nest site against other females. Ferner found that there was a high degree of male home range overlap (52%) which suggests that there is a social hierarchy rather than a territorial basis for social structure in this species. In iguanids, home ranges overlap from zero to 100%: dominance hierarchies occur at high population densities. Male home range size in *S. undulatus* decreases significantly, and the location of the home range shifts, after the breeding season. Seasonal changes in the home ranges of iguanids are not uncommon and this demonstrates a relationship between home ranges and reproductive activity.

A simple but fundamental question is, why do some species of lizards have a small home range and why do some have a large one? The relationship between home range size and lizard body weight is one possible approach to finding an answer to this fundamental question. In 1969 Turner *et al.* analysed data from 13 species of terrestrial lizards and found that the relationship between home range A (area in m^2) and body weight w (grams) could be expressed as

$$A = 171.4 \, w^{0.95}$$

It is tempting to suggest that larger lizards have greater daily energy requirements than small lizards; they would therefore require home ranges of a larger size. This would be an oversimplification and does not take into consideration abundance and availability of food, the structural nature of the habitat and foraging strategies. It is perhaps not surprising, however, to find that carnivorous lizards tend to have larger home ranges than insectivorous and herbivorous forms.

Many studies have shown that the home range and territory characteristics of lizards are determined mainly by reproductive requirements and in part by food and foraging requirements. This might suggest that immature lizards do not have home ranges and move randomly about the habitat. There is a paucity of studies on young lizards, but work by Simon and Middendorf (1980) on juvenile *Sceloporus jarrovi* has produced results which suggest that home ranges and/or territories are established close to birth locations and that, for this species, territorial behaviour began at an early age.

There is little good evidence to suggest that snakes have territories, but many studies have shown that snakes do have home ranges (sometimes called "limited movement areas"). A few species have no recognizable home range and move about in a random fashion. For those species which do have a home range, there is often a considerable difference between the mean size of the male and the female home range. The structure of the habitat and the availability of the resources influence the size of home ranges within a population and between species, but in general it seems that larger snake species have larger home ranges.

6.4   Mortality and life tables

In simple terms, the size of a population is determined by natality and mortality: if the population is stable, then natality and mortality will be equal. Mortality schedules of a population of lizards can conveniently be described in the form of a life table, and provided sufficient data are available, the average net reproductive rate (R_0) can be calculated. Few studies of reptiles are so complete that useful life table information can be obtained, but some studies on lizards have provided information useful to the analysis of population dynamics of the species; for example, Tinkle and Ballinger (1972) described the intraspecific comparative demography of the lizard *Sceloporus undulatus* (Table 6.1). The authors concluded that with the exception of the data for the Ohio population, the rates of replacement indicate that all populations are able to maintain at least a stable population size; that is, multiply by a factor of 1.14 or 1.05 in each generation. It is suggested that the low R_0 for the Ohio population is due to the difficulty of recapturing hatchlings in significant numbers. Differences in life tables between these populations are as great as those observed between species, and Tinkle and Ballinger suggest that differences in survivorship and life expectancy are due to differences in predation in these populations—a suggestion for which there is indirect evidence.

The results of this, and later work on life tables of lizards has led to the general belief that lizard adult life expectancy is generally inversely correlated with the frequency of clutches produced in a single season, or the reproductive effort. That is, long-lived species will tend to have a low

Table 6.1 Life tables for *Sceloporus undulatus* from (A) South Carolina population, (B) Texas population and (C) Ohio population. From Tinkle and Ballinger (1972) *Ecology*, **53**, 570–584.

	Age class (x)	Survivorship (l_x)	Fecundity (m_x)	Product $(l_x m_x)$
A	0	1.00	0	0
	0.25	0.31	0	0
	0.83	0.11	5.0	0.55
	1.83	0.04	8.4	0.34
	2.83	0.02	8.4	0.17
	3.83	0.01	8.4	0.08
				$R_0 = 1.14$
B	x	l_x	m_x	$l_x m_x$
	0	1.00	0	0
	0.25	0.80	0	0
	0.75	0.06	14.3	0.86
	1.75	0.01	19.5	0.19
				$R_0 = 1.05$
C	x	l_x	m_x	$l_x m_x$
	0	1.00	0	0
	0.25	0.49	0	0
	0.75	0.08	0	0
	1.75	0.03	11.8	0.35
	2.75	0.01	13.0	0.13
	3.75	0.01	13.0	0.13
				$R_0 = 0.61$

x = age class or age group; first, female eggs, second, age at hatching, third and subsequent are midpoints of seasons.

l_x = probability of surviving from first age class to midpoint of age class over which m_x is measured.

m_x = number of female offspring (eggs) produced by each adult female aged x per time unit (one reproductive season). This value for each age class was determined from clutch size and clutch frequency.

R_0 = replacement rate per generation.

annual reproductive effort. Natality balances mortality in a stable population, but in addition both the density and biomass of the population will be limited by the availability of resources. We would therefore expect that some mechanisms operate to prevent the over-exploitation of resources. Some of these mechanisms will act in response to the density of the population, while others will act independently of the density of the population. For example, Philibosian (1975) describing research on territorial behaviour and population regulation in two *Anolis* species, concluded that the territory requirements of one species (*A. cristatellus*) limit the density of breeding populations. This species has a large territory requirement and it was found that the territories could not be reduced when the population was experimentally increased. The ecologically similar species *A. acutus* is able to tolerate much smaller territories and it has been suggested that egg and juvenile mortality may limit the population of this species.

The impact of predation on the population dynamics of lizards has not been well researched, and there are still many aspects to be investigated, for example: (1) do lizard populations respond to predation by increasing fecundity or by increasing adult survivorship; (2) are the predators selective and therefore take lizards which if they were to survive would contribute little to reproduction; (3) do the predators have a direct density-dependent effect on the prey population? Comparative population studies such as that by Parker and Pianka (1975) on the lizard *Uta stansburiana* have attempted to answer some of these questions. They found, for example, that northern populations of this species produce fewer clutches and few offspring per year, responding primarily to climatic factors, while southern populations of the same species produce numerous clutches and numerous progeny each year responding to biotic factors particularly predation and competition.

6.5   Niche and resources

The 1970's brought a flurry of research activity on reptile habitat preferences, niche segregation and resource partitioning in communities. Both the *Anolis* lizards and many desert lizards have been the subject of this kind of investigation. It is perhaps not surprising that a high species richness amongst *Anolis* lizards and the desert lizards has made them attractive groups for studies on habitat selection and resource partitioning (see Pianka *et al.*, 1979, for reviews of the literature). A question common to all this research has been: what factors enable many species of lizards to coexist?

Work on the feeding ecology and food preferences of congeneric sympatric species has probably contributed much to the early ideas on partitioning of resources. It has often been observed that sympatric species of lizards tend to eat different types of prey, but of course it does not necessarily follow that the sympatric species under examination are avoiding competition for food, simply by selection of different prey types; habitat differences, temporal differences in foraging activity, and differences in foraging strategies might provide equally plausible explanations. Food is but one resource, therefore partitioning of resources can occur along habitat dimensions, temporal dimensions and also in relation to specific aspects of the habitat, such as basking sites. The resemblance between the ecology of two or more coexisting species, and the extent to which they reach equilibrium with their resources, has resulted in the term "niche" being used in a wide variety of ways.

A popular definition of an ecological niche is "the activity range of each species along every dimension of the (abiotic and biotic) environment" (Hutchinson, 1959). Each of these dimensions can be thought of as a dimension in space. If there are n dimensions, the niche is described in an n-dimensional space, of which it occupies a certain defined volume. The concept of niche breadth (width or size) has been found to be particularly useful. A measure of niche breadth requires first some identification of niche dimensions. In the case of reptiles a niche dimension would logically include type of prey eaten, size of prey eaten, time of activity, and microhabitat preference, such as perch height in *Anolis* lizards. Niche breadth can be quantified by use of a diversity index such as Simpson's (1949):

$$B = \frac{1}{\sum\limits_{i=1}^{n} (Pi)^2}$$

where B = the breadth, n = number of different resources, Pi = the frequency of utilization of the ith category. For example, a lizard's prey might consist of 10% beetles, 40% ants and 50% spiders: the niche breadth on this one dimension would be:

$$B = \frac{1}{(0.10)^2 + (0.40)^2 + (0.50)^2}$$

$$= 2.38.$$

In a community where several species share or compete for some resource, there would predictably be some dissimilarity between species along one dimension. Research along these lines has produced a number of useful concepts, such as the principle of competitive exclusion, species packing and maximal tolerable niche overlap (Pianka *et al.*, 1979). In communities where more than one dimension is utilized, similarity of

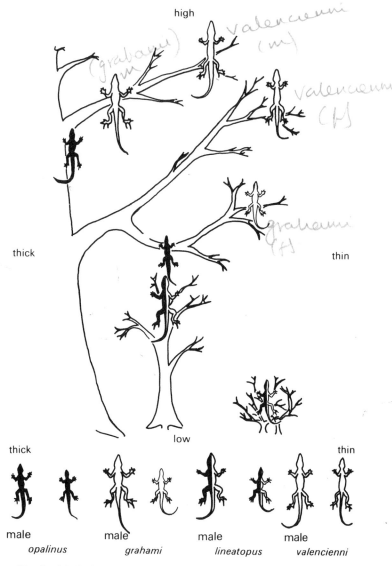

thick

thin

thick   thin

low

thick   thin

male   male   male   male

opalinus   *grahami*   *lineatopus*   *valencienni*

Figure 6.2   Spatial distribution of some *Anolis* lizards. Bottom line of lizards shows how a direct relation between perch diameter and lizard size within species and an inverse relation between species, results in those classes of different species adjacent in perch diameter being of maximally different size. Actual spatial placement of lizards is shown above. Sizes scaled according to actual mean sizes. Fully shaded = found mostly in shaded places, unshaded = found mostly in sunny places. Redrawn from Schoener, T. W. (1974) *Science*, **185**, 27–39.

species along one dimension should imply dissimilarity along another dimension if the resources are to be distinct. Schoener (1974) examined the spatial separation of four *Anolis* lizards to see how they coped with competition for food (small insects). The four lizards show an inverse correlation between body size and perch diameter (Figure 6.2) (large lizards are able to use small thin perches because they have an elongated body form with short-femured limbs). Also, the species break down into classes: adult females are usually considerably smaller than adult males. Within species, larger individuals use larger perches. The spatial arrangement (Figure 6.2) is such that there is a *direct* relation between perch diameter and lizard size within species, but an *inverse* relation between species and perch size. It was found that lizard size is distributed in space so as to minimize resource overlaps between species. Results from this study on *Anolis* lizards show how one resource might be divided between individuals and species. The next logical step in the analysis would be to determine which dimensions are important for the separation of species. Are species evenly distributed in niche space or are there guilds (similar species with similar ecologies)?

Niche relationships between two or more potentially competing species can be examined by looking at niche overlap. Niche overlap does not necessarily imply competition, because competition also depends on resource quantity and on population levels. Niche overlap along a single dimension may also not give a true picture of real overlap when the animal's true use of multidimensional niche space is considered. For example two sympatric lizard species with the same prey preference may forage at different times or may forage at different levels in the vegetation.

Mathematical bases of three commonly used measures of niche overlap along a single resource dimension have been described by Slobodchikoff and Schulz (1980). For example, niche overlap (O_{jk}) for each pair of species can be measured using a symmetrical expression as suggested by Pianka (1973):

$$O_{jk} = \frac{\sum_{i=1}^{n} Pij\,Pik}{\sum Pij^2 \, \sum Pik^2}$$

where Pij and Pik are Pi values for species j and k respectively. O_{jk} varies from 0 (no overlap) to 1 (total overlap). A good example of how niche breadth and niche overlap are analysed can be found in the study of diet overlap in three sympatric species of garter snakes (*Thamnophis*) by Gregory (1978). The niche breadth and the niche overlap for the three

Table 6.2 Niche breadth and niche overlap for three species of *Thamnophis*. From Gregory, P. T. (1978) *Can. J. Ecol.*, **56**, 1967–1974.

Food type	T. sirtalis fi	T. sirtalis Pi	T. ordinoides fi	T. ordinoides Pi	T. elegans fi	T. elegans Pi
Amphibians	41	0.612			2	0.015
Earthworms	24	0.358	67	0.515	5	0.038
Slugs			63	0.485	60	0.458
Fish					41	0.313
Mammals					17	0.130
Birds	1	0.015			2	0.015
Leeches	1	0.015				
Reptiles					4	0.031
Σ	67	1.000	130	1.000	131	1.000
B	1.987		1.998		3.054	
O_{jk}		0.367				
			0.057			
					0.597	

Mean $0 = 0.340$, f = absolute frequency, Pi = proportion of all resources actually used, which is made up of resource i. Other symbols as in text.

species are shown in Table 6.2. As diet is the only dimension considered, this research is really a first step in a study of niche overlap. Nevertheless we can see that *T. ordinoides* has a comparatively narrow food preference and that overlap on this one dimension occurs least between the two species *T. sirtalis* and *T. elegans*.

The next step is to examine several niche dimensions simultaneously. Schoener (1974) showed that pairs of species of *Anolis* with high overlap in diet tend to separate in their use of microhabitats (Figure 6.3). Pairs using similar microhabitats overlap relatively little in the size of the prey. A multidimensional analysis of niche separation and resource utilization would be more useful than an analysis where one or two dimensions are considered. The complexity of both the resources and the lizard's ecology makes this a very difficult, but not impossible, problem to solve (Slobodchikoff and Schulz, 1980).

In Chapter 3, general differences between lizard communities in western Australian deserts and North American deserts were described. The concepts of niche and niche breadth provide a basis for an empirical analysis of the association between species richness and niche breadth. Is there greater niche overlap or narrower niche breadth in communities with

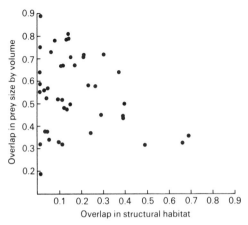

Figure 6.3 Similarity in prey size plotted against similarity in structural microhabitat among various species of *Anolis* lizards. Pairs with high dietary overlap tend to exploit different structural microhabitats. Redrawn from Schoener, T. W. (1974) (see Figure 6.2).

a high species richness? Does species richness correlate with species packing? Pianka has examined lizard communities in three areas, North America, the western Australian deserts and the Kalahari desert of southern Africa (Pianka and Huey, 1978; Pianka *et al.*, 1979). He calculated niche breadths for the resources of time, microhabitat and food, but found that niche breadths do not appear to vary with the species richness in each community. He did find however, that in the more diverse Australian communities, diet overlap was less than in North American and African communities. Australian geckos, for example, consume a substantially greater variety of prey items. Distribution of overlap in microhabitats was not found to differ significantly. Pianka concluded that the major factor associated with the higher species richness of Australian geckos is their consumption of a greater variety of prey. For example, the overall size of the food niche space used by geckos is greater in Australia.

Differences between reptile communities can usefully be described in terms of niche separation and resource utilization. Communities are dynamic systems and so we would expect to find evidence of shifts in the niche. One way to investigate displacement or niche shift would be to record the animal's behaviour and morphological characteristics. This kind of datum can be considered as a mirror of the animal's niche. That is, we might predict that for sympatric species-pairs, there would be an evolutionary divergence in morphological and behavioural characters used in the utilization of resources. Huey *et al.* (1974) found character displacement in fossorial viviparous skinks (*Typhlosaurus*) of the Kalahari. Two partially sympatric species (*T. lineatus* and *T. gariepensis*), making up sympatric populations of *T. lineatus* and *T. gariepensis* and allopatric populations of *T. lineatus*, were examined. Morphologically sympatric *T. lineatus* were larger than those of allopatric *T. lineatus*. This species also differed from *T. gariepensis* in being larger and possessing a larger head. Both species have one brood per year but the mean litter size of *T. lineatus* was 1.6 compared with 1.0 for *T. gariepensis*. Offspring of sympatric *T. lineatus* were significantly heavier than those of allopatric females and fewer sympatric *T. lineatus* females were reproductive than allopatric females. Both species were found to feed on termites, but differences were found between species in the species and caste of termite taken. Prey size differences paralleled lizard size differences. Huey *et al.* concluded that because of dietary shifts by *T. lineatus* in sympatry, the dietary overlap with *T. gariepensis* is reduced for (at least) the females and the immature lizards. There seems to be good evidence to show that character shifts are probably not related to differences in habitats between allopatry and sympatry, nor to reproductive strategies. Morphological and dietary evidence supports the idea (for *T. lineatus* females and immature lizards) that behavioural and morphological character displacement has occurred reducing dietary overlap with *T. gariepensis*.

The importance of voluntary temperatures for reptiles has been emphasized in Chapter 5, and it was also noted that some reptiles have a very broad range between the voluntary minimum and the voluntary maximum. Reptiles of this kind would be eurythermal. It might be expected that eurythermal reptiles have a broad habitat preference. The ecology of at least one *Anolis* lizard indicates that this kind of relationship does occur. The lizard *Anolis oculatus*, an endemic solitary anole of Dominica, does not seem to have any specific range of body temperatures for activity. Ruibal and Philibosian (1970) have found that this species occupies diverse habitats and that it is tempting to relate eurythermy with a wide niche breadth, at least for the one-dimensional microhabitat. Some of the anoles of the Greater Antilles have narrow voluntary temperature ranges, and Ruibal and Philibosian suggest that interspecific competition limits the spatial niche of these species and consequently limits the range of environmental temperatures available to these lizards. Further investigations based on an analysis of niche dimensions of *A. oculatus* and related species may indeed show that there is a real connection between eurythermy and niche breadth.

Research on competition and niche characteristics of reptiles will, without any doubt, continue to provide valuable ideas and lead to a better understanding of how communities have evolved and how they function. Much of the research in this area is theoretical; nevertheless there have been some recent and valuable contributions which are based on field-work. The recent discussion on guild structure in lizards by Pianka (1980) is particularly valuable in this respect. Based on an astonishing 12 person-years' collection of data, Pianka's results are an inspiration to any field herpetologist. It may be possible to quantify guild structure and therefore begin to understand its effect on the structure and diversity of reptilian and other communities. Much of Pianka's discussion is speculative. Nevertheless he asks a number of most interesting questions and suggests some equally interesting ideas—for example, that guild structure may foster diversity by means of competitive mutualisms arising from the indirect effects between species that belong to different guilds.

CHAPTER SEVEN

BEHAVIOUR

7.1 Ethology of reptiles

Chelonians, in both temperate and tropical latitudes, have an annual cycle of activity which centres around their seasonal nesting behaviour. The annual cycles of marine turtles, especially the green turtle (*Chelonia mydas*) and the hawksbill turtle (*Eretmochelys imbricata*), are spectacular in this respect, with migrations of between 1–2000 km between the feeding grounds and the nesting beaches. Seasonal movements and dispersal patterns of young sea turtles, compared to those of adults, are poorly understood and the term "lost year" has been adopted to emphasize this gap in information and consequent need for further research.

In addition to annual cycles, diurnal (possibly lunar) rhythms are also important aspects of chelonian rhythmic behaviour. Most tortoises are diurnally active, with basking and foraging occurring as regular components of daily behaviour. The few exceptions to diurnally active tortoises include *Terrapene ornata* and hatchlings of marine species such as *Chelonia mydas*. Nocturnal movements of the latter are thought to reduce the impact of predation and avoid the high daytime temperature of the nesting beaches.

Communication between conspecifics includes olfaction, vocalizations (in some species), posturing (head movements, open mouth displays) and of more importance, tactile stimuli (Auffenberg, 1977). During courtship, males of many tortoise species will bump, ram and bite the female, and in some instances there may be surprisingly active, but brief, periods of trailing behaviour.

In marine species, copulation occurs at the water surface and is sometimes preceded by group behaviour where several males actively swim alongside or with the female. Because both sexes have smooth wet surfaces at the time of mating, it is necessary for the male to hook the thumb claw of each flipper over the female's carapace on to the soft parts between the female's neck and shoulder. Mating in terrestrial species, particularly those with a high domed carapace, appears somewhat strenuous. Mounting is facilitated by the concave plastron of the male; support is then provided by long front claws and the recurved tail which is thrust forward to appose the female's tail. Most species lay eggs in cavities which they have dug, and nest building behaviour can in some species be both prolonged and elaborate. For example, the green turtle spends more time on average than other sea turtles when nesting, and the nest construction, egg laying and covering of the eggs and nest may involve several stages. After emerging from the nest, hatchlings are very often subjected to immense predation pressures; synchronous hatching within and between nests may however diminish the impact of predation.

The tuatara (*Sphenodon*) is active mainly at night and shares a close association with marine birds, such as petrels. For about four months of the year (April to mid-August) they will not feed and remain in their burrows. Only when the temperature is above 10°C will they emerge and forage for food. During much of the day they sit motionless and bask at the entrance to the burrow, but at night they feed actively on beetles, crickets, snails and nocturnal geckos. Detection of prey seems to be mainly by sight rather than by olfaction (Dawbin, 1962). The vocal repertoire of the tuatara consists of loud short croaks and low growls, the latter possibly being associated with mating displays although little is known about courtship behaviour. Eggs are laid between October and December. Between eight and fourteen eggs are deposited in shallow depressions, then covered with soil, and incubation usually takes thirteen or fourteen months. Shortly after the young emerge they are at least as active as small lizards, yet adult tuataras are often reported to be slow moving and somewhat sluggish in their behaviour.

Lizards have been the subject of extensive behavioural studies. Circadian rhythms of behaviour are found in many species and the majority are day-active. The large thermophilous agamids, varanids and chamaeleons are all decidedly diurnal, mainly because of high body temperature requirements. Many lizards including the geckos, xantusiids and *Heloderma* are, in contrast, inactive during the day and emerge only at twilight or at night. Circadian behaviour of lizards has been much investigated and in most species changes in light intensity and temperature levels are used as reference points or "zeitgebers" for phase adjustment.

Behaviour of conspecific lizards, particularly the diurnal forms, has been studied more closely than in any reptile group. Methods of communication include olfaction, vocalization, posturing and physical contact — geckos are well known for their vocalizations and some have local names which are onomatopoetically derived. At least seven other lizard families (Chamaeleonidae, Iguanidae, Lacertidae, Pygopodidae, Scincidae, Teiidae and Varanidae) include vocalizing species, although only a few, such as some *Anolis* species, have been studied in depth (Milton and Jenssen, 1979). Many species in the families Anguidae and Scincidae possess structural and behavioural specializations that relate to olfaction, suggesting that this is the dominant means of communication. The iguanids and the agamids, by contrast, have elaborate repertoires of social behaviour, mostly of visual significance. One behaviour inventory for an iguanid (*Anolis carolinensis*) contains 47 behavioural patterns associated with social interactions (Greenberg, 1977).

Aggressive behaviour between rival males is particularly spectacular in the agamids. A large number of elements of behaviour have been identified and the most common include open mouth displays, head bobbing, circling, biting and clashing head on, with attempts to push each other backwards. Fighting between male lizards may, in some species, include prolonged physical contact interrupted by brief periods when the dominant individual chases its opponent. Tail thrashing and tail biting are common elements of lizard behaviour, and in some species the incidence of tail breaks may be linked to territorial aggressive encounters. The level of aggressive behaviour varies markedly between species, a phenomenon which has led to a suggestion that there is an inverse relationship between adult life expectancy and degree of aggressiveness.

The onset of the breeding season can in some lizard species be identified by changes in skin colour. This prenuptial coloration, as with behaviour posturing, may facilitate sex recognition. Possession of a territory can be an important prerequisite for attracting a mate and the territories of some lizard species are used for mating, nesting, and egg laying as well as for feeding (Brattstrom, 1974). The timing, duration and intensity of courtship and other lizard social behaviour can be affected by changes in local weather conditions. This is perhaps not surprising, particularly as social behaviour (like other behaviour) does not occur below a certain body temperature threshold. Stamps (1976), in a study of the social behaviour of the lizard *Anolis aeneus*, found that the number of lizards active at study sites and the display frequencies varied inversely with days since rainfall, suggesting that rainfall as well as temperature can affect social behaviour.

Because lizard social behaviour and thermoregulatory behaviour are both affected by abiotic factors, there is possibly a conflict between these two activities. Avery (1976) noted that amongst European lacertids, behavioural complexity decreases with progressive northwards extension of their range, possibly because diurnal heliothermic lizards in temperate climates must devote a considerable part of their activity period to behavioural thermoregulation. This observation is well worth further investigation.

Nesting behaviour in one lacertid species (*Lacerta agilis*) has been examined in detail (House and Spellerberg, 1981) and the results of this investigation have shown that the females actively look for sites which will be optimal for rapid and successful incubation of the eggs. Sites with high insolation but which contained moist soil were found to be favoured. There was evidence to suggest that the presence of fine, living roots in the vicinity of the nest may promote a constant humid environment, and that these roots were detected by the lizards during their search for a nest site.

The response of lizards to predators includes threat displays, cryptic behaviour and escape. Threat displays are varied (inflation of the body, guttural hissing and other vocalizations, open mouth and tongue displays) and perhaps the most unusual is the ability of some horned lizards (*Phrynosoma*) to squirt blood from their eyelids. There are a few lizards which may have a mimetic resemblance to snakes, including the legless lizard *Anguis fragilis* (Smith, 1974) and members of the genus *Pygopus* (Bustard, 1968).

Prior to recent reports by Cloudsley-Thompson (1977) and Gans (1978) very little was known about the biology and behaviour of the Amphisbaenia or worm lizards. Well modified for burrowing and a fossorial existence, the amphisbaenians utilize rectilinear locomotion which depends upon a flexible integument that can telescope along part of the circumference. The Trogonophidae use their convexly curved snout to assist when digging burrows whereas the Bipedidae use their over-developed forelimbs to initiate entry into tunnels. Moist soil is preferred by these animals and they use their long tunnels when foraging for food. Movement and olfactory cues are used when looking for food and they readily respond to the movement of small insects. There is conflicting evidence regarding their ability to absorb water through the integument but it is interesting to note that they do obtain water by drinking. Without doubt it would be most rewarding to investigate fully the behaviour, particularly the reproductive behaviour, of these most fascinating reptiles.

Many snakes have an annual activity pattern of behaviour which is linked either to levels of food abundance or to seasonal changes in temperature. For example, the primary factor stimulating emergence from wintering sites is temperature, although light cycles may be an additional cue for some species. Studies of daily activity patterns in snakes have also shown that both temperature and light cycles are the main factors controlling this form of behaviour. On a daily basis, increasing temperatures will induce commencement of activity in many species, but above certain temperature thresholds activity may be depressed. Certain temperature cycles may also result in a change from a monophasic to a diphasic pattern of activity (Heckrotte, 1962; Spellerberg and Phelps, 1977).

The role of the tongue and Jacobson's organ in the detection and trail following of prey has been well analysed (see 7.3), but less attention has been devoted to the behavioural aspects of prey location. Snakes in general employ both searching and sit-and-wait strategies and a few species (e.g. the water snake, *Natrix sipedon*) may adopt a specific "searching image". Porter and Czaplicki (1977) found that under certain circumstances, members of this species which have had experience in capturing cryptic prey will adopt a specific searching image whereby prey which are coloured similarly to their background are more readily captured than are conspicuous prey. Whereas some snakes actively search for prey, some employ tail lures. This behaviour occurs in aquatic, terrestrial, and arboreal forms such as coral snakes (*Micruroides euryxanthus*), death adders (*Acanthophis antarcticus*) and the python (*Chondropython viridis*). The behaviour of snakes when holding and overpowering prey includes simple seizing, seizing and holding with one coil, poisoning and constricting. The constricting method is particularly vigorous in the Boidae, whereas colubrids constrict in a less vigorous and less predictable fashion (Willard, 1977).

Communication between conspecific snakes entails olfactory and tactile stimuli. Behavioural encounters between male conspecifics consist typically of entwining and twisting of the mid- to posterior trunk regions and tails, followed by attempts to force each other to the ground. Male combat rituals may involve high vertical display stances (crotalines) to horizontal stances (colubrids) with either male attempting to force the other's head down (Carpenter, 1977). Snakes with vestigial posterior appendages, such as found in some of the boids, employ their spurs during combat bouts as well as in courtship behaviour.

Sex recognition in some snakes is facilitated by the use of chemical cues (pheromones). For example, the male adder (*Vipera berus*) is able to detect and follow the chemical trail left by a female over distances of several kilometres. In general, male snakes are far more active than females during courtship and mating. Elements of courtship and mating behaviour include chasing, entwining, parallel alignment, chin rubbing, rippling movements of the trunk wall, and biting. Obviously the synchronization of cloacal gaping is a prerequisite for successful mating and for this, tactile communication seems particularly important.

The response of snakes to predators is usually rapid escape, but in some species it includes defence and attack. Some, such as the water snake *Natrix natrix*, feign death when confronted with a predator, while others such as the hognose snake (*Heterodon nasicus*), also exhibit self-wounding displays (Kroll, 1977). Colour patterns in some snake species seem to be strongly influenced by selection for predator avoidance (Jackson *et al.*, 1976). Mimicry in snakes is widely accepted, but mainly on the basis of supposition rather than on empirical evidence (Kroon, 1975).

In general, the diurnal behaviour of crocodilians has two main components, basking and foraging for food. The duration and temporal aspects of crocodile daily behaviour depend largely on local temperature cycles. For example, the Nile crocodile (*Crocodylus niloticus*) spends the night in the water and generally there are two basking periods during the day; one in the early morning and the other during mid-afternoon. The pattern of movement between water and land in this, and in other species, results in a fairly constant body temperature.

The hearing capacity of crocodiles is superior to other reptiles and so it is not unexpected to find that vocalizations are well developed. Young crocodiles vocalize as they hatch and in many species the parents may respond to the calls of the piping young. Vocalizations of adult crocodilians occur in connection with individual and sex recognition, group cohesion, mating, warning and distress calls (Staton, 1978). This vocal repertoire supports the conclusion that many of the crocodilians have an elaborate social behaviour. In some species, territorial defence may include tail displays, inflated postures, narial geysering (a spout of water rising from the nares), and head slapping (Garrick and Lang, 1977). Courtship behaviour in some crocodilians includes bellowing choruses, mutual snout contacts and possibly olfactory communication.

Crocodilian nests are varied in their degree of structural complexity: some species excavate a simple hole for the eggs, others construct mounds of vegetation. In all species studied so far it has been found that behaviour associated with nesting, egg laying and care of the young is complex and sometimes elaborate. Defence of the nest, liberation of the hatchlings and post-hatching care have been described for a number of species (Deitz and Hines, 1980).

7.2 Patterns of behaviour

Research on animal behaviour is often directed towards an understanding of either the biological basis, or the elements of behaviour. The biological basis of behaviour includes genetic inheritance, learning, motivation and physiological states. A number of elements of behaviour are readily identified; for example, there is the reflex or a chain of reflexes where the stimulus always elicits the same response. For instance, in those reptiles with movable eyelids, the irritation caused by an object on the cornea causes the nictitating membrane to sweep across the reptile's eye, clearing and lubricating the surface. Relationships among elements such as the releaser (sign stimulus) and fixed action patterns, can be demonstrated by examining the displays of agamid lizards. Males of some *Amphibolurus* species when resident in a territory will, for example, respond to the presence of an intruding male (releaser) by a fixed action pattern of behaviour, including lowering of the gular region, lateral alignment, leg rotation and tail coiling. The fixed action pattern is a sequence of co-ordinated motor actions that are performed without learning. Some patterns of behaviour occur in connection with a motivational state such as hunger. Patterns of feeding behaviour of a snake may include appetitive or searching behaviour, and consummatory behaviour, terminating in quiescence because of the change in motivation state. Patterns of behaviour such as these provide a useful basis for a better understanding of the ontogeny, causation and function and evolutionary aspects of behaviour.

Rhythmic patterns of behaviour are of particular importance during migration. It has been found in a wide range of taxa, including reptiles, that the position of a celestial body is used as a directional cue. To be effective in migration there must be time compensation to allow for the movement of the celestial bodies, otherwise the animal's migratory movements would follow an arc across the earth's surface. In some species it has been found that this time compensation is controlled by a biological clock, and takes the form of an endogenous rhythm. Gourley (1974) has described time-compensated solar orientation in the tortoise *Gopherus polyphemus* in open fields and in an arena that excluded landmarks. When the activity cycle of this species was phase-shifted by six hours, the characteristic 90° shift in preferred direction was obtained, indicating that *G. polyphemus* is capable of time-compensated solar orientation.

The body temperature of a reptile is largely the result of its behaviour. A few species seem able to increase their body temperature as a result of metabolic heat production at times of aggressive displays (Engbretson and Livezey, 1972). But is it correct to assume that patterns of behaviour result in regulation and control of temperature? If the body temperature of a reptile is controlled and regulated by behaviour, then we should be able to predict various forms of behaviour—that is, does a reptile respond to changes in the thermal environment in a predictable manner? Bartlett and Gates (1967) examined the positions of a lizard (*Sceloporus occidentalis*) on a tree trunk and calculated the lizard's energy budget throughout the day. If the lizard was to maintain its body temperature within a certain range,

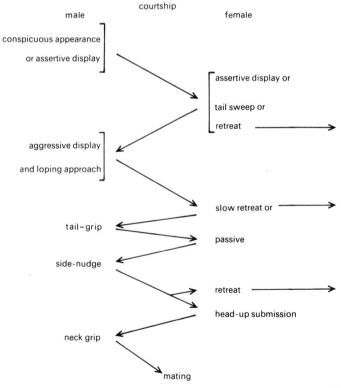

Figure 7.1 Courtship in the lizard *Sceloporus cyanogenys*: idealized sequence of typical behaviour patterns. Redrawn from Greenberg, N. (1977) *J. Herpetol.*, **11**, 177–195.

then it should change its position on the tree trunk throughout the day in a predictable manner. By making detailed calculations of the lizard's energy budget it was possible for Bartlett and Gates to obtain a good agreement between the predicted positions of the lizard and those observed. Thus in this lizard certain patterns of behaviour do result in the control and regulation of the animal's body temperature.

Patterns of courtship behaviour can be very complex, and therefore it is sometimes difficult to portray the sequence of events in a meaningful way. The ethogram provides a precise way in which to catalogue the behaviour patterns of animals and ethograms are often used to describe complexities of courtship behaviour. One example (Figure 7.1) comes from the detailed laboratory studies of the blue spiny lizard, *Sceloporus cyanogenys*, by Greenberg (1977). Courtship in this species commences when the male detects and responds to an intruder in his territory. A female would make herself conspicuous, either by performing an assertive display (pushups and head nods), or by swinging her tail in a broad arc. The male may then move towards the female and respond aggressively (pushups and head nods) or adopt a loping approach (body movements up and down in a sinuous pattern, tail up and down and relatively fast forward movement). Females, even those that had formerly displayed a tail lash, might try to retreat at this point, but more often a female would move only slightly. When a male is close enough to shift to lateral orientation, an attempt to escape may elicit pursuit, the male often successfully obtaining a tail-grip on the female. The male may allow the female to lead him around. Females subjected to this gentle restraint sometimes turn around towards the male and effect a release by a side-nudge, but more often they become passive and remain still in a posture of body down-alert with head up. The male will now work along the female's body with side nudges until he approaches the neck area. There is much nudging around the neck until, facilitated by the female's head-up posture, he establishes a neck-grip. Copulation is accomplished when the male, alongside the female, places the rear leg nearest the female over her pelvic area so that he appears to be partly resting on her back. These sequences of behaviour lend themselves to ethogram analysis and also to quantification (i.e. the most common sequence can be predicted).

7.3 Analysis of reptile behaviour

Analysis of tongue-flicking frequency in snakes and investigations of the nature and the function of the vomeronasal organs are two methods used to study chemoreception in snakes. For example, a simple technique used in the analysis of the response of snakes to chemical cues is to obtain chemical extracts from different prey items, then to record frequency of tongue flicking when the chemical stimulus is presented to the snakes. Using this approach it has been found that newborn snakes have genetic pre-dispositions for certain prey items, and that the response of adult snakes can be modified by previous diet (Arnold, 1978). This kind of information on the overt behaviour of the snake is very relevant to our understanding of how snakes seek, select, and capture their prey. Studies other than at whole animal level are also important for the analysis of behaviour. Isolation of the neural and hormonal correlates of chemo-reception, and other neuroethological studies (Greenberg and Maclean, 1977) are particularly relevant, although space here does not permit an account of these aspects.

It is often difficult to demonstrate cause and effect in animal behaviour and one interesting way by which this problem can be overcome is worthy of mention. James and Porter (1979) used principal component analysis for identification of a subset of variables, which demonstrated relation-ships between lizard behaviour and abiotic factors. Two particularly important variables were soil surface temperature and net radiation. When

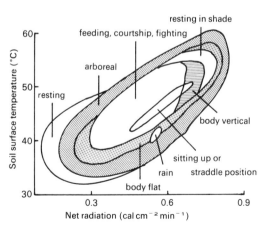

Figure 7.2 Summary of behavioural data for the lizard *Agama agama*. These data (for a week) are plotted in the time-independent space of values for soil surface temperature and net radiation. Behavioural events for the nine days were superimposed and lines drawn to define their spatial pattern. To read radiation in watts, insert 2.1×10^{-2}, 4.2×10^{-2} and 6.3×10^{-2} along the abscissa. Redrawn from James, F. C. and Porter, W. P. (1979) *Copeia*, 1979, 585–593.

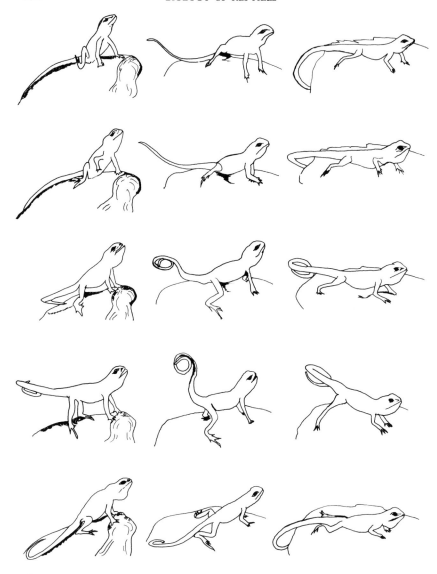

Figure 7.3 Hind leg pushup display of the *Amphibolurus decresii* species complex. Representation from each phase of the hind leg pushup display in *A. fionni* (left column), *A. vadnappa* (middle column) and *A. decresii* (right column). Top row, preliminary posture. Second row, leg rotation in phase one. Middle row, beginning of hind leg extension in phase two. Fourth row, full extension. Bottom row, head dip position in phase three. Redrawn from Gibbons, J. R. H. (1979) *Copeia*, 1979, 29–40.

behavioural data are plotted in a space determined by these variables, the activities fall into a pattern (Figure 7.2). In this graph, which is a simple bivariate plot of two variables, it can be seen that the complex behaviour of the lizard occurs in a surprisingly orderly fashion. From data of this kind it is then possible to predict behavioural events from information about the thermal environment, and to test whether or not seasonal social patterns are in any way constrained by the microclimate.

Displays of lizards have not until recently been analysed in an attempt to determine the extent and nature of interspecific differences in congeneric species. In 1979, Gibbons analysed pushup displays in three species of *Amphibolurus* with the aim of using ethological criteria to test morphological classification. The *Amphibolurus decresii* complex is restricted to South Australia, and apart from the coloration of adult males, all three species look similar. Considerable variation was found to occur both at populational and species levels in elements of the territorial pushup displays (Figure 7.3). One element of this display, coiling of the tail, was found to be a good taxonomic criterion. In *A. decresii*, coiling of the tail was always in a horizontal plane, and in *A. vadnappa* it was always vertical. In *A. fionni* the tail was coiled in a similar way to *A. decresii*, but was held less rigidly and often in an oblique plane. Classification of the lizards according to these and other display characteristics complemented a recent revision of the *A. decresii* complex on a morphometric basis.

Reptiles have not been used extensively in the field of experimental behaviour. Simple techniques for teaching lizards to perform visual discrimination tasks have been outlined by Loop (1976) and operant conditioning procedures have been used to investigate thermoregulatory behaviour. From research of this kind it has been found that body temperature is an important parameter of learning in heliothermic reptiles (Kemp, 1969).

CHAPTER EIGHT

REPTILES AND MAN

8.1 Losses and gains

Like many other forms of wildlife, a large number of reptile species have become extinct in recent times, and many more need some form of conservation. International recognition of this fact has resulted in the publication of the third volume of the *Red Data Book* (International Union for the Conservation of Nature, 1975). Over a hundred endangered reptile species (Table 8.1) representing many families are listed in the *Red Data Book*. At least 28 reptile taxa are thought to have become extinct since 1600: of these, 36% were slaughtered for meat, and 46% became extinct through predation by feral animals or through habitat destruction (Honegger, 1981).

Table 8.1 Numbers of reptile species listed in the IUCN Red Data Book, Vol. 3

	No. of living species	No. listed and (%)
O. Chelonia		
F. Pelomedusidae	15	2 (13)
F. Chelidae	30	
F. Emydidae	80	5 (6)
F. Testudinidae	40	10 (25)
F. Platysternidae	1	
F. Chelydridae	2	
F. Kinosternidae	18	
F. Dermatemydidae	1	1 (100)
F. Cheloniidae	5	5 (100)
F. Dermochelelyidae	1	1 (100)
F. Carettochelyidae	1	1 (100)
F. Trionychidae	30	

Table 8.1—*continued*

	No. of living species	No. listed and (%)
O. Rhynchocephalia		
F. Sphenodontidae	1	1 (100)
S.O. Ophidia		
F. Anomolepidae	1	
F. Typhlopidae	200	1 (0.5)
F. Leptotyphlopidae	51	
F. Aniliidae	9	
F. Uropeltidae	44	
F. Boidae	90	9 (10)
F. Xenopeltidae	1	
F. Acrochordidae	2	
F. Colubridae	2200	6 (0.3)
F. Elapidae	200	2 (1)
F. Viperidae	150	5 (3)
O. Crocodylidae	21	19 (90)
S.O. Lacertilia		
F. Gekkonidae	580	5 (1)
F. Pygopodidae	23	
F. Xantasiidae	6	1 (19)
F. Dibamidae	3	
F. Anelytropsidae	1	
F. Iguanidae	680	20 (5)
F. Agamidae	315	1 (0.5)
F. Chamaeleontidae	109	
F. Scincidae	700	3 (0.5)
F. Lacertidae	164	2 (1)
F. Teiidae	210	2 (1)
F. Feylinidae	4	
F. Cordylidae	47	
F. Anguidae	88	1 (1)
F. Anniellidae	2	1 (50)
F. Xenosauridae	4	
F. Varanidae	30	2 (7)
F. Helodermatidae	2	2 (100)
F. Lanthanotidae	1	
S.O. Amphisbaenia	130	

The population status of many reptile species has diminished not because of direct exploitation but because of losses in their habitat. In heavily populated areas such as some parts of Britain there are many demands on the land for all reasons, often culminating in the loss and fragmentation of safe wildlife habitats. So great have been the losses of reptile habitats in Britain that some nature reserves have been established mainly for the rare reptiles.

Seemingly minor uses of land have also had an impact on reptile habitats. For example Busack and Bury (1974) describe how, in the Mojave Desert of California, both grazing and off-road-vehicles ("dune buggies") result in irreparable damage to wildlife communities, and particularly the reptile communities. Other environmental impacts such as thermal pollution can however enhance reptile habitats. In 1974 Christy *et al.* reported increased growth rates and body size of turtles living in thermal and post-thermal aquatic systems adjacent to atomic energy plants, and in the same year Murphy and Brisbin described how American alligators (*A. mississippiensis*) made use of heated areas in a reactor cooling reservoir.

The habitats of some reptile species have been extended or modified as a result of man's activities. For example, the construction of stone walls in areas of central Europe has probably extended the habitat of some lacertid species. In southern Spain, protective boxes for electrical junctions provide shelter for two species of gecko, *Tarentola mauritanica* and *Hemidactylus turcicus*. The distribution of many snake species has been extended through farming practices and in Britain the grass snake (*Natrix natrix*) has extended its northern range by making use of dung and grass heaps where the eggs are deposited and incubated.

It is not surprising that some reptile species have been introduced (by design or by accident) to some countries and have become established exotics. As a result of legislation protecting American alligators in the early 1950's, the number of caimans imported into the United States, primarily for the pet trade, increased. By 1960 feral caimans (*Caiman crocodilus*) from central South America had become established in the Miami area canal system and now they are very much part of the Florida herpetofauna (Ellis, 1980). Britain has a comparatively rich introduced reptile fauna with some well-established (but not widespread) species such as the European pond tortoise (*Emys orbicularis*) and the common wall lizard *Podarcis muralis*.

8.2   Reptiles as a resource

The exploitation of chelonian and crocodilian species for food and for leather products has been well documented. Records as early as 1700 describe the importance of turtles for meat and eggs to sailors of the time. For 300 years the green turtle (*Chelonia mydas*) of the Caribbean has been exploited for its meat (also turtle soup) and this species has been regrettably over-exploited, as have many other marine animals. Kemp's ridley (*Lepidochelys kempi*), is now restricted to one population found only on a single beach in Mexico, and is but one turtle which is near extinction. Once counted in tens of thousands, there are only a few hundred breeding females remaining. Turtle eggs have also been prized as food. Once the part of local people's diet, turtle eggs have been the target of many over-enthusiastic commercial ventures.

The magnificent great land tortoises of the Galapagos Islands have also served as a food source for buccaneers but more recently have been over-exploited. About 5000 giant tortoises were taken over a period of thirty years early in the 19th century: later in the same century they were to become extinct on some of the Galapagos Islands. Today, feral animals add to the threats facing the giant tortoises.

Many other reptiles are exploited for food, and some species are considered to be a delicacy—rattlesnake meat is much sought-after in parts of the United States. A West Indian iguana has the sad but apt specific name *delicatissima*, because, like other iguanids, it is sold for consumption. Sea snakes are fished commercially in the Philippines, mainly for their skins, but also for animal and human consumption (Punay, 1975).

Turtles have long been commercially valuable and the combined effects of over-exploitation and economic demand have sometimes led to the establishment of turtle farming or, more correctly, management of wild populations. For example, in 1968 the world's first turtle farm commenced activities at the Grand Cayman Island in the British West Indies (Bustard, 1972). Reliance on hatchery-reared turtles rather than on natural popula-tions was desired and there has been some success in attempts to combine management, culling, and farming techniques. In general, however, management of wild turtle populations has not been economically successful. Management necessarily involves human interference and this can have a deleterious effect. Despite rigorous conditions it has been found that the hatching success of turtle eggs can be seriously decreased following efforts to manage incubation processes (Harless and Morlock, 1979; Pritchard, 1980).

Successful harvesting of reptile populations depends on a good know-ledge of their ecology and behaviour. Information on reproductive rates, survival rates of different age-classes, population dynamics, and food requirements are all relevant but unfortunately these aspects of the animal's biology have not been fully investigated. Small changes in temperature can, for example, make considerable differences to the sex ratio of hatchling sea turtles. In 1980 Mrosovsky and Yntema concluded that incubation of sea turtle eggs under artificial conditions can result in a sex ratio in favour of either females or males: for freshwater snapping turtles (*Chelydra serpentina*) there are more females at higher temperatures and more males at lower temperatures. Habitats critical for the survival of a species need further research—one example of work in the right direction is that by Lazell (1980), who has presented evidence to show the importance of New England waters for the leatherback turtle (*Dermochelys*

Table 8.2 Testudinidae and Iguanidae imported into Britain and declared purpose of importation (%)

Year	Total imported	Exhibition (zoos and breeding)	Scientific research	Pets	Resale
A. Testudinidae (including Emydidae)					
1965	235 913*	0.002	0.24	0.03	99.7
1966	224 573*	0.007	—	0.02	99.8
1967	419 876*	0.02	0.001	0.02	99.9
1968	223 172	0.004	0.003	0.01	99.9
1969	180 940	0.01	0.007	0.03	99.9
1970	275 066	0.001	0.001	0.02	99.9
1971	222 950	0.001	0.05	0.02	99.9
1972	267 685	0.008	1.39	0.006	98.5
1973	114 223	0.02	0.09	0.02	99.9
1974	97 639	0.01	0.002	0.06	99.9
1975	180 873	0.003	27.33	0.023	72.6
B. Iguanidae					
1965	3 334*	0.67	0.50	—	98.8
1966	2 978*	0.26	1.53	—	98.2
1967	536*	2.35	—	0.26	97.4
1968	472	2.16	—	—	97.8
1969	1 087	0.82	0.37	0.37	98.4
1970	1 237	0.97	—	—	99.0
1971	1 279	0.86	2.8	0.08	96.1
1972	1 293	2.16	1.54	0.31	95.9
1973	748	1.74	1.34	0.13	96.8
1974	1 571	1.5	—	3.3	95.2
1975	833	0.24	5.51	—	94.2

* These figures are estimated from the numbers licensed. Between 1965 and 1967 the information is incomplete and although it is not always possible to make an accurate assessment between the numbers imported and numbers licensed it seems that about 70% of reptiles for which licences were granted were actually imported. The 11th and final report of the Advisory Committee set up under the Animals (Restriction of Importation) Act 1964 gave figures for 1975. Modified from Spellerberg, I. F. (1976) *Biol. Cons.*, **10**, 221–232.

coriacea) and other marine species. Between August and November the largest known concentrations of the leatherback in the Atlantic occur in these waters. Aspects of this area of sea salient to the ecology of the species need further research so as to provide further information for good management.

8.3 Reptiles and the pet trade

Collection of reptiles for the pet trade has possibly been as devastating as the exploitation of populations for food and leather products. In the United States vast numbers of young tortoises, crocodiles, lizards and snakes are sold as pets: over 99 % of crocodile imports are destined for the pet trade (King, 1974). An indication of the extent of reptile imports into Britain has been derived from reports (Departments of Education and Science, Department of the Environment) of the Advisory Committee on the Animals (Restriction of Importation) Act 1964 (Table 8.2). Figures for the period 1965–1975 have been made available; in January 1976 the Act was suspended when the controls implementing the Convention on International Trade in Endangered Species of Wild Flora and Fauna were introduced into the United Kingdom. The figures in Table 8.2 are informative, but in addition there have been reports showing that some species have dramatically declined as a result of collecting. Allen (1974) has reported a decrease in green lizard (*Lacerta viridis*) populations (France) and eyed lizard (*Lacerta lepida*) populations (Portugal) based on studies since 1966. Lambert (1969, 1980) drew attention to the impact of tortoise collecting and has recorded sparse populations in some areas of Morocco. Collecting of the spur-thighed tortoise (*Testudo graeca*) in large numbers for the pet trade and as local souvenirs has had a dramatic impact on local tortoise populations (Honegger, 1974). In more general terms, trade in European reptiles has led to such a decline in populations that 47 species (45 % of those currently recognized) are in more or less immediate danger of extinction.

8.4 Reptiles in education, research and conservation

The culture and maintenance of reptiles in zoological gardens not only provides an education facility but has also been the basis for considerable advances in herpetology (see for example Phelps, 1981). Volume 19 of the *International Zoo Year Book* includes 29 articles on reptiles, good evidence of the role of captive reptiles in research (Olney, 1979). Applied aspects of herpetological research should not go unnoticed. In 1975 Bauerle *et al.* put forward a good case for the use of snakes as indicators of levels of pollution. As carnivores, snakes could usefully be used in studies on the impact of herbicides, pesticides and lead in the natural environment. Medica *et al.* (1973) have concerned themselves with the effects of continuous radiation exposure on lizards and have discussed both direct and indirect evidence of radiation-induced sterility among female horned lizards (*Phrynosoma platyrhinos*).

The success of efforts to conserve reptiles depends largely on good and regular monitoring of populations in the field. Information then needs to be collated and distributed to those active in the efforts of conservation. A publication of considerable importance to reptile conservation is *Endangered and Threatened Amphibians and Reptiles in the United States*, compiled by R. E. Ashton (Edwards and Pisani, 1976). The lists of threatened and endangered reptiles are important in themselves, but equally important are the attempts by the contributors to identify the specific causes of habitat destruction and to recommend conservation methods.

Knowledge of a reptile species' requirements (heat, food, space etc.) can also improve conservation methods. One requirement, space, has been extensively examined in relation to lizard ecology in both Australia and Britain. Kitchener *et al.* (1980) examined 23 reserves in Western Australia to evaluate their adequacy for conservation of lizards. It was concluded that relationships between area and lizard species richness for wheatbelt reserves are very similar to those for comparable continental island lizard faunas. Although lizard richness was found to be strongly correlated with the number of plant associations, there was less correlation with number of plant species and plant formations. It has been possible for these authors to suggest an optimum size for lizard reserves, but they note that some of the smaller reserves contained some of the more infrequently collected lizard species in the region. Research on the habitat requirements of the sand lizard (*Lacerta agilis*) in Britain, a species once widely distributed in southern England but now represented by small fragmented populations, has shown that area requirements are very much modified by the ecology of the area. Sparse populations of this lizard survive in areas of open heathland (areas in which the dominant life form is that of an ericoid dwarf-shrub and where trees or dwarf shrubs are absent), whereas high population densities are supported in sites undergoing succession from ericoid shrub associations to grassland or woodland (House and Spellerberg, 1982).

The deliberate release of a species into an area to which it was indigenous in historical times (i.e. reintroduction) is one method which has been used in attempts to conserve reptiles but with little or no success. Although ecologically versatile lizards should be easy to reintroduce, the rare and endangered species, often with more restricted requirements, may not be suitable for this kind of management. The breeding of reptiles in captivity with the aim of reintroducing them is another method which has yet to be fully researched. There seem to be advantages in conducting such programmes in the field and the work on the Galapagos giant tortoise is noteworthy in this respect (Macfarland et al., 1974). Eight of 11 surviving races of Galapagos tortoises (*Geochelone elephantopus*) are threatened due to decreased population sizes and predation and/or competition by introduced mammals. While methods are being developed for the reduction of pressures brought about by the introduced mammals, young of the endangered races of giant tortoises are being hatched and raised in captivity for restocking of endemic populations. These authors have developed highly successful techniques for establishment of breeding colonies, incubation of eggs, and raising of young in captivity, and such efforts contribute a great deal to the conservation of this reptile species.

Captive breeding of endangered reptile species is being successfully carried out in a number of zoos—the splendid work of the Jersey Wildlife Preservation Trust is well worth noting. Round Island in the Mauritian archipelago has a unique reptile fauna, but goats and rabbits on the islands have destroyed the habitats of these reptiles. Specimens of the Round Island skink (*Leiolopisma telfairii*), Round Island gecko (*Phelsuma guentheri*), and Round Island boa (*Casarea dussumieri*) have been collected for captive breeding at Jersey Zoo. In two years, 80 skinks and 24 geckos have been hatched, and the Round Island boa (possibly the world's rarest snake) has recently started to breed in captivity. Plans to restore the vegetation on Round Island are under way and it may soon be possible to reintroduce these unique reptiles.

8.5 Reptiles and wildlife legislation

A few noteworthy reptiles have been legally protected for many years: for example the tuatara (*Sphenodon*) of New Zealand (since 1907), and the Gila monster (*Heloderma*) of Arizona (since 1952). More recently some countries have passed laws to protect at least part of their indigenous reptile fauna. In Switzerland all species of amphibians and reptiles (and their habitats) have been protected by law since 1966; Germany protects all its lizard and most snake species, and Poland also has given legal protection to its reptile fauna. The legislative protection of some British species was enacted in 1975 and more recently in 1981 (the Wildlife and Countryside Act). In the United States, the Endangered Species Act of 1973 provides a means whereby wildlife (including reptiles) and the habitat necessary for their survival may be protected. Many individual states in the United States have their own laws for the protection of local reptile species, and Dodd's (1979) bibliography of endangered herpetofauna in the US confirms the widespread interest in conservation of reptiles.

Probably the most important landmark in the protection of reptiles (and other wildlife) occurred when the International Union for the Conservation of Nature (IUCN) initiated restriction in trade of rare animals. To date about 60 countries have signed the 1973 Convention of Trade in Endangered Species of Wild Fauna and Flora: the UK has been implementing this since 1976. The Convention aims to protect, by means of international co-operation, certain species of wild animals and plants from over-exploitation through international trade.

For many species of reptile, it is the habitat rather than the species which needs to be safeguarded. As in the case of thousands of species of wild animals and plants, the changes in land use by man have resulted in the fragmentation of reptile populations and so the status of many species has declined. There is good justification for the special protection of certain reptiles but all too often this taxon has received much less attention than other taxa such as birds and mammals. It is to be hoped that the strategies for international action proposed in the World Conservation Strategy (IUCN, 1980) will have a significant part to play in safeguarding the habitats of reptiles and other wildlife.

BIBLIOGRAPHY

Chapter 1

Camin, J. H. and Ehrlich, P. R. (1958) Natural selection in water snakes (*Natrix sipedon* L.) on islands in Lake Erie. *Evolution*, **12**, 504–511.

Carroll, R. L. (1969) "Origins of reptiles", in *Biology of the Reptilia*, Vol. 1, ed. Gans, C., Bellairs, A. d'A. and Parsons, T. S., Academic Press, London and New York, pp. 1–44.

Clover, R. C. (1979) Phenetic relationships among populations of *Podarcis sicula* and *P. melisellensis* (Sauria: Lacertidae) from islands in the Adriatic Sea. *Syst. Zool.*, **28**, 284–298.

Colbert, E. H. (1965) *The Age of Reptiles*. Weidenfeld and Nicolson, London.

Dietz, R. S. and Holden, J. C. (1970) The breakup of Pangaea. *Scient. Amer.*, **223**, 30–41.

Dunson, W. A. (1975) *The Biology of Sea Snakes*. University Park Press, Baltimore.

Francis, E. T. B. (1977) Amphisbaenia: heart and arterial arches. *Brit. J. Herpetol.*, **5**, 607–610.

Gans, C. (1978) The characteristics and affinities of the Amphisbaenia. *Trans. Zool. Soc., London*, **34**, 347–416.

Ginsburg, L. (1970) "Les reptiles fossiles", in *Traité de Zoologie*, Vol. 14, Reptiles, ed. Grasse, P. P., Masson, Paris, pp. 1161–1332.

Gorman, G. C., Wilson, A. C. and Nakonishi, M. (1971) A biochemical approach towards the study of reptilian phylogeny: evolution of serum albumin and lactic dehydrogenase. *Syst. Zool.*, **20**, 167–185.

Matthey, R. (1970) "Les chromosomes des reptiles", in *Traité de Zoologie*, Vol. 14, Reptiles, ed. Grasse, P. P., Masson, Paris, pp. 829–858.

Molnar, R. E. and Thulborn, R. A. (1980) First Pterosaur from Australia. *Nature*, **288**, 361–363.

Olson, E. C. (1976) "The exploitation of land by early tetrapods", in *Morphology and Biology of Reptiles*, ed. Bellairs, A. d'A. and Cox, C. B., Linnean Soc. Symp. No. 3, Academic Press, London, pp. 1–30.

Romer, A. S. and Parsons, T. S. (1977) *The Vertebrate Body*. 5th ed., Saunders, Philadelphia.

Scott, P. and Rines, R. (1975) Naming the Loch Ness Monster. *Nature*, **258**, 466–468.

Swain, T. (1976) "Angiosperm-reptile co-evolution", in *Morphology and Biology of Reptiles*, ed. Bellairs, A. d'A. and Cox, B., Linnean Soc. Symp. No. 3, Academic Press, London, pp. 107–122.

Thorpe, R. S. (1980) Microevolution and taxonomy of European reptiles with particular reference to the grass snake *Natrix natrix* and the wall lizards *Podarcis sicula* and *P. melisellensis*. *Biol. J. Linn. Soc.*, **14**, 215–233.

Underwood, G. (1967) *A Contribution to the Classification of Snakes*. British Museum Pub. No. 653, British Museum, London.

Voipio, P. (1962) Multiple phaneromorphism in the European slow-worm (*Anguis fragilis*) and the distributional and evolutionary history of the species. *Ann. Zool. Soc. "Vanamo"*, **23**, 1–20.

Chapter 2

Belekhova, M. G. (1979) "Neurophysiology of the forebrain", in *Biology of the Reptilia*, Vol. 10, ed. Gans, C., Northcutt, R. G. and Ulinski, P., Academic Press, London and New York, pp. 287–359.

Bellairs, A. d'A. (1969) *The Life of Reptiles*. (2 vols.) Weidenfeld and Nicolson, London.

Bücherl, W., Buckley, E. and Deulofeu, V. (1968–71) *Venomous Animals and their Venoms*. (3 vols.) Academic Press, New York and London.

Bullock, T. H. and Cowles, R. B. (1952) Physiology of an infrared receptor: the facial pit of pit vipers. *Science*, **115**, 541–543.

Buning, T. J. de Cock, Poelmann, R. E. and Dullemeijer, P. (1978) Feeding behaviour and the morphology of the thermoreceptors in *Python reticulatus*. *Netherlands J. of Zoology*, **28**, 62–93.

Bustard, H. R. (1968) Temperature dependent tail autotomy mechanism in gekkonid lizards. *Herpetologica*, **24**, 127–130.

Davies, P. M. C., Patterson, J. W. and Bennett, E. L. (1980) "The thermal ecology, physiology and behaviour of the viperine snake, *Natrix maura*: some preliminary observations", in *European Herpetological Symposium 1980*, ed. Coborn, J., Cotswold Wildlife Park Ltd., Oxford, pp. 107–116.

Derickson, W. K. (1976) Lipid storage and utilization in reptiles. *Amer. Zool.*, **16**, 711–723.

Dhouailly, D. (1975) Formation of cutaneous appendages in dermo-epidermal recombinations between reptiles, birds and mammals. *Wilhelm Roux's Archives*, **177**, 323–340.

Florkin, M. and Scheer, B. T. (1974) *Chemical Zoology*, Vol. 9, Amphibia and Reptilia, Academic Press, New York and London.

Fox, W. (1963) Special tubules for sperm storage in female lizards. *Nature*, **198**, 500–501.

Gans, C. (1952) The functional morphology of the egg-eating adaptations in the snake genus *Dasypeltis*. *Zoologica, N.Y.*, **37**, 209–244.

Gans, C. (1962) Terrestrial locomotion without limbs. *Am. Zool.*, **2**, 167–182.

Godley, J. S. (1980) Foraging ecology of the striped swamp snake, *Regina alleni*, in southern Florida. *Ecol. Monog.*, **50**, 411–436.

Goldby, F. and Gamble, H. J. (1957) The reptilian cerebral hemispheres. *Biol. Rev.*, **32**, 383–420.

Gundy, G. C., Ralph, C. L. and Wurst, G. Z. (1975) Parietal eyes in lizards: zoogeographical correlates. *Science*, **190**, 671–672.

Halpern, M. and Kubie, J. L. (1980) Chemical access to the vomeronasal organs of garter snakes. *Physiol. and Behav.*, **24**, 367–371.

Iordansky, N. N. (1973) "The skull of the Crocodilia", in *Biology of the Reptilia*, Vol. 4, ed. Gans, C. and Parsons, T. S., Academic Press, London and New York, pp. 201–263.

Johnson, R. N. and Lillywhite, H. B. (1979) Digestive efficiency of the omnivorous lizard *Klauberina riversiana*. *Copeia*, 1979, 431–437.

Kochva, E. (1978) "Oral glands of the Reptilia", in *Biology of the Reptilia*, Vol. 8, ed. Gans, C. and Gans, K. A., Academic Press, London and New York, pp. 43–162.

Krebs, J. R. and Davies, N. B. (1978) *Behavioural Ecology*. Blackwell, Oxford.

Maderson, P. F. A. (1965) Histological changes in the epidermis of snakes during the sloughing cycle. *J. Zool., London*, **146**, 98–113.

Nagy, K. A. (1977) Cellulose digestion and nutrient assimilation in *Sauromalus obesus*, a plant-eating lizard. *Copeia*, 1977, 355–362.

Parker, H. W. (1965 & 1977) *Snakes: A Natural History* (2nd ed.) revised by Grandison, A. G. C., British Museum and Cornell Univ. Press, London and Ithaca.

Quay, W. B. (1979) "The parietal eye-pineal complex", in *Biology of the Reptilia*, Vol. 9, ed. Gans, C., Northcutt, R. G. and Ulinski, P., Academic Press, London and New York, pp. 245–406.

Regal, P. J. (1975) The evolutionary origins of feathers. *Quart. Rev. Biol.*, **50**, 35–66.

Romer, A. S. (1956) *Osteology of the Reptiles*. Univ. Chicago Press, Chicago.

Savitzky, A. H. (1981) Hinged teeth in snakes: an adaptation for swallowing hard-bodied prey. *Science*, **212**, 346–349.

Simpson, S. B. (1965) "Regeneration of the lizard tail", in *Regeneration in Animals and Related Problems*, ed. Kiortsis, V. and Trampusch, H. A. L., North-Holland Pub. Co., Amsterdam, pp. 431–443.

Skoczylas, R. (1978) "Physiology of the digestive tract", in *Biology of the Reptilia*, Vol. 8, ed. Gans, C. and Gans, K. A., Academic Press, London and New York, pp. 589–717.

Smith, G. C. (1976) Ecological energetics of three species of ectothermic vertebrates. *Ecology*, **57**, 252–264.

Snyder, R. C. (1962) Adaptations for bipedal locomotion of lizards. *Am. Zool.*, **2**, 191–203.

Underwood, H. and Menaker, M. (1970) Extraretinal light perception: entrainment of the biological clock controlling lizard locomotor activity. *Science*, **170**, 190–193.

Vitt, L. J., Congdon, J. D. and Dickson, N. A. (1977) Adaptive strategies and energetics of tail autotomy in lizards. *Ecology*, **58**, 326–337.

Wever, E. G. and Vernon, J. A. (1960) The problem of hearing in snakes. *J. Aud. Res.*, **1**, 77–83.

Wever, E. G. (1979) *The Reptile Ear*. Princeton University Press.

Chapter 3
Beebee, T. J. C. (1978) An attempt to explain the distributions of the rare herptiles *Bufo calamita, Lacerta agilis*, and *Coronella austriaca* in Britain. *Brit. J. Herpetol.*, **5**, 763–770.

Darlington, P. J. (1957) *Zoogeography: the Geographical Distribution of Animals*. John Wiley, New York.

Dobzhansky, T. (1950) Evolution in the tropics. *Am. Scient.*, **38**, 209–221.

Dunson, W. A. (1975) *The Biology of Sea Snakes*. Univ. Park Press, Baltimore.

Etheridge, R. (1960) The relationships of the anoles (Reptilia: Sauria: Iguanidae): on interpretations based on skeletal morphology. Ph.D. Thesis, University Microfilms, Inc., Ann Arbor, Michigan.

Gans, C. (1979) The characteristics and affinities of the Amphisbaenia. *Trans. zool. Soc. Lond.*, **34**, 347–416.

Gorman, G. C. and Atkins, L. (1969) The zoogeography of Lesser Antillean *Anolis* lizards—an analysis based upon chromosomes and lactic dehydrogenases. *Bull. Mus. Comp. Zool.*, **138**, 53–80.

Gorman, G. C. and Dessauer, H. C. (1965) Hemoglobin and transferrin electrophoresis and relationships of island populations of *Anolis* lizards. *Science*, **150**, 1454–1455.

MacArthur, R. H. (1972) *Geographical Ecology*. Harper and Row, New York.

MacArthur, R. H. and Wilson, E. O. (1967) *The Theory of Island Biogeography*. Princeton University Press, Princeton.

Mao, S. H. and Chen, B. Y. (1980) *Sea Snakes of Taiwan: a Natural History of Sea Snakes*, NSC Special Pub., No. 4, N.S.C., Taiwan.

Pianka, E. R. (1966) Latitudinal gradients in species diversity: a review of concepts. *Am. Nat.*, **100**, 33–46.

Pianka, E. R. (1967) On lizard species diversity: North American flatland deserts. *Ecology*, **48**, 333–351.

Pianka, E. R. (1969) Habitat specificity, speciation, and species density in Australian desert lizards. *Ecology*, **50**, 498–502.

Pianka, E. R. (1977) "Reptilian species diversity", in *Biology of the Reptilia*, Vol. 7, ed. Gans, C. and Tinkle, D. W., Academic Press, London and New York, pp. 1–34.

Sill, W. D. (1968) The zoogeography of the Crocodilia. *Copeia*, 1968, 76–88.

Webb, J. E., Wallwork, J. A. and Elgood, J. H. (1978) *Guide to Living Reptiles*. Macmillan Press Ltd., London.

Wilcox, B. A. (1980) "Insular ecology and conservation", in *Conservation Biology*, ed. Soule, M. E. and Wilcox, B. A., Sinauer Associates Inc., Massachusetts, pp. 95–117.

Williams, E. E. (1969) The ecology of colonization as seen in the zoogeography of anoline lizards on small islands. *Quart. Rev. Biol.*, **44**, 345–389.

Yalden, D. W. (1980) An alternative explanation of the distributions of the rare herptiles in Britain. *Brit. J. Herpetol.*, **6**, 37–41.

Chapter 4

Andrews, R. and Rand, A. S. (1974) Reproductive effort in anoline lizards. *Ecology*, **55**, 1317–1327.

Auffenberg, W. and Iverson, J. B. (1979) "Demography of terrestrial turtles", in *Turtles, Perspectives and Research*, ed. Harless, M. and Morlock, H., John Wiley and Sons, New York, pp. 541–569.

Avery, R. A. (1975) Clutch size and reproductive effort in the lizard *Lacerta vivipara* Jacquin. *Oecologia*, **19**, 165–170.

Badham, J. A. (1971) Albumen formation in eggs of the agamid *Amphibolurus barbatus barbutus*. *Copeia*, 1971, 543–545.

Bellairs, R. (1971) *Developmental Processes in Higher Vertebrates*. Logos Press Ltd., London.

Berry, J. F. and Shine, R. (1980) Sexual size dimorphism and sexual selection in turtles (order Testudines). *Oecologia*, **44**, 185–191.

Castanet, J. (1978) Les marques de croissance osseuse comme indicateurs de l'âge chez les lézards. *Acta Zool.*, **59**, 35–48.

Chapman, B. M. and Chapman, R. F. (1964) Observations on the biology of the lizard *Agama agama* in Ghana. *Proc. Zool. Soc., London*, **143**, 121–132.

Crews, D. (1975) Psychobiology of reptilian reproduction. *Science*, **189**, 1059–1065.

Cuellar, O. (1971) Reproduction and the mechanism of meiotic restitution in the parthenogenetic lizard, *Cnemidophorus uniparens*. *J. Morph.*, **133**, 139–165.

Darevsky, I. S. (1966) Natural parthenogenesis in a polymorphic group of caucasian rock lizards related to *Lacerta saxicola* Eversmann. *J. Ohio Herpetol. Soc.*, **5**, 115–152.

Devine, M. C. (1975) Copulatory plugs in snakes: enforced chastity. *Science*, **187**, 844–845.

Dufaure, J. P. and Hubert, J. (1961) Table de développement du lézard vivipare: *Lacerta* (*Zootoca*) *vivipara* Jacquin. *Arch. d'Anat. Micr. Morph. Exp.*, **50**, 309–327.

Fitch, H. S. (1970) *Reproductive Cycles of Lizards and Snakes*. Univ. Kansas Mus. Nat. Hist. Misc. Pub. No. 52, Museum of Natural History, Univ. of Kansas.

Gibbons, J. W. (1976) "Aging phenomena in reptiles", in *Special Review of Experimental Aging Research*, ed. Elias, M. F., Eleftheriou, B. E. and Elias, P. K., Progress in Biology, EAR, Inc., Maine, pp. 454–475.

Gibbons, J. W. and Nelson, D. H. (1978) The evolutionary significance of delayed emergence from the nest by hatchling turtles. *Evolution*, **32**, 297–303.

Inger, R. F. and Greenberg, B. (1966) Annual reproductive patterns of lizards from a Bornean rain forest. *Ecology*, **47**, 1007–1021.

Kellerway, L. G. and Brain, P. F. (1978) A preliminary study on seasonal variations in testicular function in the viper (*Vipera berus* L.): a histological investigation. *IRCS Med. Sci.*, **6**, 94.

Lamb, M. J. (1977) *Biology of Ageing*. Blackie, Glasgow and London.

Licht, P. (1971) Regulation of the annual testis cycle by photoperiod and temperature in the lizard *Anolis carolinensis*. *Ecology*, **52**, 240–252.

Pasteels, J. J. (1970) "Développement embryonnaire", in *Traité de Zoologie*, Vol. 14, Reptiles, ed. Grasse, P. P., Masson, Paris, pp. 893–971.

Porter, K. R. (1972) *Herpetology*. W. B. Saunders Co., London.

Prestt, I. (1971) An ecological study of the viper *Vipera berus* in southern Britain. *J. Zool., London*, **164**, 373–418.

Reese, A. M. (1915) *The Alligator and its Allies*. G. P. Putnam and Sons, New York.

Shine, R. (1980) Costs of reproduction in reptiles. *Oecologia*, **46**, 92–100.

Stonehouse, B. (1978) *Animal Marking*. Macmillan, London.

Tinkle, D. W. and Gibbons, J. W. (1977) *The Distribution and Evolution of Viviparity in Reptiles.* Misc. Pub. Mus. Zool. Univ. Mich., No. 154.

Tinkle, D. W. and Hadley, N. F. (1975) Lizard reproductive effort: caloric estimates and comments on its evolution. *Ecology*, **56**, 427–434.

Tinkle, D. W. and Irwin, L. N. (1965) Lizard reproduction: refractory period and response to warmth in *Uta stansburiana* females. *Science*, **148**, 1613–1614.

Tinkle, D. W., Wilbur, H. M. and Tilley, S. G. (1970) Evolutionary strategies in lizard reproduction. *Evolution*, **24**, 55–74.

Turner, F. B. (1977) "The dynamics of populations of squamates, crocodilians and rhynchocephalians", in *Biology of the Reptilia*, ed. Gans, C. and Tinkle, D. W., Academic Press, London and New York, pp. 157–264.

Williams, G. C. (1966) *Adaptation and Natural Selection.* Princeton University Press, Princeton, New Jersey.

Wright, J. W. and Lowe, C. H. (1968) Weeds, polyploids, parthenogenesis and the geographical and ecological distribution of all-female species of *Cnemidophorus*. *Copeia*, 1968, 128–138.

Yntema, C. L. (1968) A series of stages in the embryonic development of *Chelydra serpentina*. *J. Morph.*, **125**, 219–252.

Zehr, D. R. (1962) Stages in the normal development of the common garter snake *Thamnophis sirtalis sirtalis*. *Copeia*, 1962, 322–329.

Chapter 5

Aleksiuk, M. (1971) Temperature-dependent shifts in the metabolism of a cool temperate reptile, *Thamnophis sirtalis parietalis*. *Comp. Biochem. Physiol.*, **39A**, 495–503.

Avery, R. A. (1979) *Lizards—a Study in Thermoregulation*. Studies in Biology, No. 109, Edward Arnold, London.

Bartholomew, G. A. (1968 & 1977) "Body temperature and energy metabolism", in *Animal Function: Principles and Adaptations*, (3rd ed.), ed. Gordon, M. S., Bartholomew, G. A., Grinnell, A. D., Jorgensen, C. B. and White, F. N., Collier MacMillan, London, pp. 364–448.

Bartholomew, G. A. and Lasiewski, R. C. (1965) Heating and cooling rates, heart rate and simulated diving in the Galapagos marine iguana. *Comp. Biochem. Physiol.*, **16**, 573–583.

Clarke, D. R. (1973) Temperature responses of three Costa Rican lizards (*Anolis*). *Carib. J. Sci.*, **13**, 199–206.

Cloudsley-Thompson, J. L. (1971) *The Temperature and Water Relations of Reptiles.* Merrow Pub. Co. Ltd., Watford, England.

Cloudsley-Thompson, J. L. (1972) "Temperature regulation in desert reptiles", in *Comparative Physiology of Desert Animals*, ed. Maloiy, G. M. O., *Symp. Zool. Soc. Lond.*, **31**, Academic Press, London, pp. 39–59.

Cloudsley-Thompson, J. L. and Butt, D. K. (1977) Thermal balance in the tortoise and its relevance to dinosaur extinction. *Brit. J. Herpetol.*, **5**, 641–647.

Cowles, R. B. and Bogert, C. (1944) A preliminary study of the thermal requirements of desert reptiles. *Bull. Am. Mus. nat. Hist.*, **83**, 265–296.

Dantzler, W. H. and Holmes, W. N. (1974) "Water and mineral metabolism in Reptilia", in *Chemical Zoology*, Vol. 9, Amphibia and Reptilia, ed. Florkin, M. and Scheer, B. T., Academic Press, New York and London, pp. 277–336.

Davies, P. M. C. and Bennett, E. L. (1981) Non-acclimatory latitude-dependent metabolic adaptations to temperature in juvenile natricine snakes. *J. Comp. Physiol.*, **142**, 489–494.

De Witt, C. B. (1967) Precision of thermoregulation and its relation to environmental factors in the desert iguana, *Dipsosaurus dorsalis*. *Physiol. Zool.*, **40**, 49–66.

Dutton, R. H. and Fitzpatrick, L. C. (1975) Metabolic compensation to seasonal temperatures in the rusty lizard, *Sceloporus olivaceus*. *Comp. Biochem. Physiol.*, **51A**, 309–318.

Girgis, S. (1961) Aquatic respiration in the common Nile turtle, *Trionyx triunguis* (Forskål). *Comp. Biochem. Physiol.*, **3**, 206–217.

Greenwald, D. E. (1974) Thermal dependence of striking and prey capture by gopher snakes. *Copeia*, 1974, 141–148.

Greer, A. E. (1980) Critical thermal maximum temperatures in Australian scincid lizards: their ecological and evolutionary significance. *Aust. J. Zool.*, **28**, 91–102.

Heath, J. E. (1964) Reptilian thermoregulation: evaluation of field studies. *Science*, **146**, 784–785.

Heatwole, H. (1976) *Reptile Ecology*. University of Queensland Press, St Lucia.

Jackson, D. C. (1979) "Respiration", in *Turtles, Perspectives and Research*, ed. Harless, M. and Morlock, H., John Wiley and Sons, New York, pp. 165–191.

Lee, J. C. (1980) Comparative thermal ecology of two lizards. *Oecologia*, **44**, 171–176.

Licht, P. (1965) The relation between preferred body temperatures and testicular heat sensitivity in lizards. *Copeia*, 1965, 428–436.

Licht, P. and Bennett, A. F. (1972) Tests of the role of reptilian scales in water loss and heat transfer. *Copeia*, 1972, 702–707.

Mierop, van, L. H. S. and Barnard, S. M. (1976) Thermoregulation in a brooding female python *Molurus bivittatus* (Serpentes: Boidae). *Copeia*, 1976, 398–401.

Mrosovsky, N. and Pritchard, P. C. H. (1971) Body temperatures of *Dermochelys coriacea* and other sea turtles. *Copeia*, 1971, 624–631.

Munsey, L. D. (1972) Water loss in five species of lizards. *Comp. Biochem. Physiol.*, **43A**, 781–794.

Patterson, J. W. and Davies, P. M. C. (1978) Thermal acclimation in temperate lizards. *Nature*, **275**, 646–647.

Philpott, C. W. and Templeton, J. R. (1964) A comparative study of the histology and fine structure of the nasal salt secreting gland of the lizard, *Dipsosaurus*. *Anat. Rec.*, **148**, 394–395.

Pollock, M. and MacAvoy, E. S. (1978) Morphological and metabolic changes in muscles of hibernating lizards. *Copeia*, 1978, 412–416.

Pough, F. H. (1973) Heart rate, breathing and voluntary diving of the elephant trunk snake, *Acrochordus javanicus*. *Comp. Biochem. Physiol.*, **44A**, 183–189.

Pough, F. H. (1976) The effect of temperature on oxygen capacity of reptile blood. *Physiol. Zool.*, **49**, 141–151.

Prosser, C. L. (1958) "General summary: the nature of physiological adaptation", in *Physiological Adaptation*, ed. Prosser, C. L., Am. Physiol. Soc., Washington, D.C., pp. 167–180.

Schmidt-Nielsen, K. (1975) *Animal Physiology, Adaptation and Environment*. Cambridge University Press, London.

Shoemaker, V. H., Licht, P. and Dawson, W. R. (1967) Thermal dependence of water and electrolyte excretion in two species of lizards. *Comp. Biochem. Physiol.*, **23**, 255–262.

Skadhauge, E. and Duvdevani, I. (1977) Cloacal absorption of NaCl and water in the lizard *Agama stellio*. *Comp. Biochem. Physiol.*, **56A**, 275–279.

Skoczylas, R. (1970) Influence of temperature on gastric digestion in the grass snake *Natrix natrix* L. *Comp. Biochem. Physiol.*, **33**, 793–804.

Spellerberg, I. F. (1972) Temperature tolerances of southeast Australian reptiles examined in relation to reptile thermoregulatory behaviour and distribution. *Oecologia*, **9**, 23–46; **9**, 371–383; **9**, 385–398; **11**, 1–16.

Spellerberg, I. F. (1976) "Adaptations of reptiles to cold", in *The Morphology and Biology of Reptiles*, ed. Bellairs, A. d'A. and Cox, C. B., Academic Press, London, pp. 261–285.

Spotila, J. R., Lommen, P. W., Bakken, G. S. and Gates, D. M. (1973) A mathematical model for body temperatures of large reptiles: implications for dinosaur ecology. *Am. Nat.*, **107**, 391–404.

Warburg, M. R. (1966) On the water economy of several Australian geckos, agamids and skinks. *Copeia*, 1966, 230–235.

Chapter 6

Bailey, N. T. J. (1952) Improvements in the interpretation of recapture data. *J. Anim. Ecol.*, **21**, 120–127.

Bustard, H. R. (1971) A population study of the eyed gecko, *Oedura ocellata* Boulenger, in northern New South Wales, Australia. *Copeia*, 1971, 658–669.

Cott, H. B. (1961) Scientific results of an enquiry into the ecology and economic status of the Nile crocodile (*Crocodilus niloticus*) in Uganda and Northern Rhodesia. *Trans. Zool. Soc. London*, **29**, 211–356.

Ferner, J. W. (1974) Home-range size and overlap in *Sceloporus undulatus erythrocheilus* (Reptilia: Iguanidae). *Copeia*, 1974, 332–337.

Gregory, P. T. (1978) Feeding habits and diet overlap of three species of garter snakes (*Thamnophis*) on Vancouver Island. *Can. J. Zoology*, **56**, 1967–1974.

Grubb, P. (1971) The growth, ecology and population structure of giant tortoises on Aldabra. *Phil. Trans. Roy. Soc. London, B*, **260**, 327–372.

Heatwole, H. (1976) *Reptile Ecology*. University of Queensland Press, St Lucia.

Huey, R. B., Pianka, E. R., Egan, M. E. and Coons, L. W. (1974) Ecological shifts in sympatry: Kalahari fossorial lizards (Typhlosaurus). *Ecology*, **55**, 304–316.

Hutchinson, G. E. (1959) Homage to Santa Rosalia, or why are there so many kinds of animals? *Am. Nat.*, **93**, 145–159.

Jennrich, R. I. and Turner, F. B. (1969) Measurement of non-circular home range. *J. Theor. Biol.*, **22**, 227–237.

Moll, E. O. and Legler, J. M. (1971) The life history of a neotropical slider turtle, *Pseudemys scripta* (Schoepff), in Panama. *Bull. Los Angeles Co. Mus. nat. Hist. Sci.*, **11**, 1–102.

Parker, W. S. and Pianka, E. R. (1975) Comparative ecology of populations of the lizard *Uta stansburiana*. *Copeia*, 1975, 615–632.

Philibosian, R. (1975) Territorial behaviour and population regulation in the lizards, *Anolis acutus* and *A. cristatellus*. *Copeia*, 1975, 428–444.

Pianka, E. R. (1973) The structure of lizard communities. *Ann. Rev. Ecol. Syst.*, **4**, 53–74.

Pianka, E. R. (1980) Guild structure in desert lizards. *Oikos*, **35**, 194–201.

Pianka, E. R. and Huey, R. B. (1978) Comparative ecology, resource utilization and niche segregation among gekkonid lizards in the southern Kalahari. *Copeia*, 1978, 691–701.

Pianka, E. R., Huey, R. B. and Lawlor, L. R. (1979) "Niche segregation in lizards", in *Analysis of Ecological Systems*, ed. Horn, D. J., Stairs, G. R. and Mitchell, R. D., Ohio State University Press, Columbus, pp. 67–115.

Plummer, M. V. (1977) Activity, habitat and population structure in the turtle, *Trionyx muticus*. *Copeia*, 1977, 431–440.

Ruibal, R. and Philibosian, R. (1970) Eurythermy and niche expansion in lizards. *Copeia*, 1970, 645–653.

Schoener, T. W. (1974) Resource partitioning in ecological communities. *Science*, **185**, 27–39.

Simon, C. A. and Middendorf, G. A. (1980) Spacing in juvenile lizards (*Sceloporus jarrovi*). *Copeia*, 1980, 141–146.

Simpson, E. H. (1949) Measurement of diversity. *Nature*, **163**, 688.

Slobodchikoff, C. N. and Schulz, W. C. (1980) Measures of niche overlap. *Ecology*, **61**, 1051–1055.

Stamps, J. A. (1977) "Social behaviour and spacing patterns in lizards", in *Biology of the Reptilia*, Vol. 7, ed. Gans, C. and Tinkle, D. W., Academic Press, London and New York, pp. 265–321.

Stickel, L. F. (1978) Changes in a box turtle population during three decades. *Copeia*, 1978, 221–225.

Tinkle, D. W. and Ballinger, R. E. (1972) *Sceloporus undulatus*: a study of the intraspecific comparative demography of a lizard. *Ecology*, **53**, 570–584.

Turner, F. B. (1977) "The dynamics of populations of squamates, crocodilians and rhynchocephalians", in *Biology of the Reptilia*, Vol. 7, ed. Gans, C. and Tinkle, D. W., Academic Press, London and New York, pp. 157–264.

Turner, F. B., Jennrich, R. I. and Weintraub, J. D. (1969) Home ranges and body size of lizards. *Ecology*, **50**, 1076–1081.

Chapter 7

Arnold, S. J. (1978) Some effects of early experience on feeding responses in the common garter snake, *Thamnophis sirtalis*. *Anim. Behav.*, **26**, 455–462.

Auffenberg, W. (1977) Display behaviour in tortoises. *Amer. Zool.*, **17**, 241–250.

Avery, R. A. (1976) "Thermoregulation, metabolism and social behaviour in Lacertidae", in *Morphology and Biology of Reptiles*, ed. Bellairs, A. d'A. and Cox, C. B., Linn. Soc. Symp. No. 3, Academic Press, London and New York, pp. 245–259.

Bartlett, P. N. and Gates, D. M. (1967) The energy budget of a lizard on a tree trunk. *Ecology*, **48**, 315–322.

Brattstrom, B. H. (1974) The evolution of reptilian social behaviour. *Am. Zool.*, **14**, 35–49.

Bustard, H. R. (1968) *Pygopus nigriceps* (Fischer): a lizard mimicking a venomous snake. *Brit. J. Herpetol.*, **4**, 22–24.

Carpenter, C. C. (1977) Communication and displays of snakes. *Amer. Zool.*, **17**, 217–223.

Cloudsley-Thompson, J. L. (1977) Some aspects of the biology of *Amphisbaena alba* L. *Brit. J. Herpetol.*, **5**, 617–621.

Dawbin, W. H. (1962) The tuatara in its natural habitat. *Endeavour*, **21**, 16–24.

Deitz, D. C. and Hines, T. C. (1980) Alligator nesting in north-central Florida. *Copeia*, 1980, 249–258.

Engbretson, G. A. and Livezey, R. L. (1972) The effects of aggressive display on body temperature in the fence lizard *Sceloporus occidentalis occidentalis* Baird and Girrard. *Physiol. Zool.*, **45**, 247–254.

Gans, C. (1978) The characteristics and affinities of the Amphisbaenia. *Trans. zool. Soc. Lond.*, **34**, 347–416.

Garrick, L. D. and Lang, J. W. (1977) Social signals and behaviour of adult alligators and crocodiles. *Amer. Zool.*, **17**, 225–239.

Gibbons, J. R. H. (1979) The hind leg pushup display of *Amphibolurus decresii* species complex (Lacertilia Agamidae). *Copeia*, 1979, 29–40.

Gourley, E. (1974) Orientation of the gopher tortoise *Gopherus polyphemus*. *Anim. Behav.*, **22**, 158–169.

Greenberg, N. (1977) An ethogram of the blue spiny lizard, *Sceloporus cyanogenys* (Reptilia, Lacertilia, Iguanidae). *J. Herpetol.*, **11**, 177–195.

Greenberg, N. and Maclean, P. D. (1977) *The Behaviour and Neurology of Lizards*. N.I.M.H., Rockville, Md.

Heckrotte, C. (1962) The effect of the environmental factors in the locomotory activity of the Plains garter snake (*Thamnophis radix radix*). *Anim. Behav.*, **10**, 193–207.

House, S. M. and Spellerberg, I. F. (1980) "Ecological factors determining the selection of egg incubation sites by *Lacerta agilis* L. in southern England", in *European Herpetological Symposium* 1980, ed. Coborn, J., Cotswold Wildlife Park, Oxford, pp. 41–54.

Jackson, J. F., Ingram, W. and Campbell, H. W. (1976) The dorsal pigmentation pattern of snakes as an antipredator strategy: a multivariate approach. *Amer. Nat.*, **110**, 1029–1053.

James, F. C. and Porter, W. P. (1979) Behaviour—microclimate relationships in the African rainbow lizard, *Agama agama*. *Copeia*, 1979, 585–593.

Kemp, F. D. (1969) Thermal reinforcement and thermoregulatory behaviour in the lizard *Dipsosaurus dorsalis*: an operant technique. *Anim. Behav.*, **17**, 446–451.

Kroll, J. C. (1977) Self-wounding while death feigning by Western hognose snakes *Heterodon nasicus*. *Copeia*, 1977, 372–373.

Kroon, C. (1975) A possible Müllerian mimetic complex among snakes. *Copeia*, 1975, 425–428.

Loop, M. S. (1976) Auto-shaping—a simple technique for teaching a lizard to perform a visual discrimination task. *Copeia*, 1976, 574–576.

Milton, T. H. and Jenssen, T. A. (1979) Description and significance of vocalizations by *Anolis grahami* (Sauria: Iguanidae). *Copeia*, 1979, 481–489.

Porter, R. H. and Czaplicki, J. A. (1977) Evidence for a specific searching image in hunting water snakes (*Natrix sipedon*) (Reptilia, Serpentes, Colubridae). *J. Herpetol.*, **11**, 213–216.

Smith, R. H. (1974) Is the slow worm a Batesian mimic? *Nature*, **247**, 571–572.

Spellerberg, I. F. and Phelps, T. E. (1977) Biology, general ecology and behaviour of the snake, *Coronella austriaca* Laurenti. *Biol. J. Linn. Soc.*, **9**, 133–164.

Stamps, J. A. (1976) Rainfall, activity and social behaviour in the lizard, *Anolis aeneus*. *Anim. Behav.*, **24**, 603–608.

Staton, M. A. (1978) Distress calls of crocodilians—whom do they benefit? *Am. Nat.* **112**, 327–332.

Willard, D. E. (1977) Constricting methods of snakes. *Copeia*, 1977, 379–382.

Chapter 8

Allen, A. (1974) Conservation, ethics, and the herpetologist. *Aquarist. Pondkpr.*, 1974, 236–237.

Bauerle, B., Spencer, D. L. and Wheeler, W. (1975) The use of snakes as a pollution indicator species. *Copeia*, 1975, 366–368.

Busack, S. D. and Bury, R. B. (1974) Some effects of off-road vehicles and sheep grazing on lizard populations in the Mojave Desert. *Biol. Conserv.*, **6**, 179–183.

Bustard, R. H. (1972) *Sea Turtles*. Collins, London and Sydney.

Christy, E. J., Farlow, J. O., Bourque, J. E. and Gibbons, J. W. (1974) "Enhanced growth and increased body size of turtles living in thermal and post-thermal aquatic systems", in *Thermal Ecology*, ed. Gibbons, J. W. and Sharitz, R. R., *AEC Sym. Ser.* (Conf. 730505), pp. 277–284.

Dodd, C. K. (1979) *A Bibliography of Endangered and Threatened Amphibians and Reptiles in the United States and its Territories*. Smithsonian Herpetological Information Service, No. 46, 35 pp.

Edwards, S. R. and Pisani, G. R. (1976) *Endangered and Threatened Amphibians and Reptiles in the United States*. Society for Study of Amphibians and Reptiles, Florida State Museum.

Ellis, T. M. (1980) *Caiman crocodilus*: an established exotic in South Florida. *Copeia*, 1980, 152–154.

Harless, M. and Morlock, H. (1979) *Turtles: Perspectives and Research*. John Wiley and Sons Inc., New York.

Honegger, R. E. (1974) Die Gefährdung der Lurche und Kriechtiere und Massnahmen für ihren Schutz: ein Zwischenbericht. *Natur. Mus.*, **104**, 280–290.

Honegger, R. E. (1981) List of amphibians and reptiles either known or thought to have become extinct since 1600. *Biol. Conserv.*, **19**, 141–158.

House, S. M. and Spellerberg, I. F. (1982) An analysis of the sand lizard (*Lacerta agilis* L.) habitat in southern England. *Biol. J. Linn. Soc.*, in press.

International Union for the Conservation of Nature (1975) *Red Data Book* 3, Amphibia and Reptilia, IUCN Morges.

International Union for the Conservation of Nature (1980) *World Conservation Strategy*. IUCN prepared with co-operation of the United Nations Environment Programme and the World Wildlife Fund.

King, F. W. (1974) Trade in live crocodilians. *Int. Zoo Yb.*, **14**, 52–56.

Kitchener, D. J., Chapman, A., Dell, J., Muir, B. G. and Palmer, M. (1980) Lizard assemblage and reserve size and structure in the Western Australian wheatbelt—some implications for conservation. *Biol. Conserv.*, **17**, 25–62.

Lambert, M. R. K. (1969) Tortoise drain in Morocco. *Oryx*, **10**, 161–166.

Lambert, M. R. K. (1980) "The Mediterranean spur-thighed tortoise, *Testudo graeca*, in the wild and in the trade", in *European Herpetological Symposium 1980*, ed. Coborn, J., Cotswold Wildlife Park, Oxford, pp. 17–23.

Lazell, J. D. (1980) New England waters: critical habitat for marine turtles. *Copeia*, 1980, 290–295.

MacFarland, G. C., Villa, J. and Toro, B. (1974) The Galapagos giant tortoises (*Geochelone elephantopus*). Part II: Conservation methods. *Biol. Conserv.*, **6**, 198–212.

Medica, P. A., Turner, F. B. and Smith, D. D. (1973) Effects of radiation on a fenced population of horned lizards (*Phrynosoma platyrhinos*) in southern Nevada. *J. Herpetol.*, **7**, 79–85.

Mrosovsky, N. and Yntema, C. L. (1980) Temperature dependence of sexual differentiation in sea turtles: implications for conservation practices. *Biol. Conserv.*, **18**, 271–280.

Murphy, T. M. and Brisbin, I. L. (1974) "Distribution of alligators in response to thermal gradients in a reactor cooling reservoir", in *Thermal Ecology*, ed. Gibbons, J. W. and Sharitz, R. R., *AEC Symp. Ser.* (Conf. 730505), pp. 313–321.

Olney, P. J. S. (1979) *International Year Book* 1979, Vol. 19, Zoological Society, London.

Phelps, T. (1981) *Poisonous Snakes*. Blandford Press, Poole, Dorset.

Pritchard, P. C. H. (1980) The conservation of sea turtles: practices and problems. *Amer. Zool.*, **20**, 609–617.

Punay, E. Y. (1975) "Commercial sea snake fisheries in the Philippines", in *The Biology of Sea Snakes*, ed. Dunson, W. A., University Park Press, Baltimore, pp. 489–502.

Index